interchange

FIFTH EDITION

3 B

Student's Book

WITH DIGITAL PACK

Jack C. Richards

with Jonathan Hull and Susan Proctor

CAMBRIDGE
UNIVERSITY PRESS

Shaftesbury Road, Cambridge CB2 8EA, United Kingdom

One Liberty Plaza, 20th Floor, New York, NY 10006, USA

477 Williamstown Road, Port Melbourne, VIC 3207, Australia

314–321, 3rd Floor, Plot 3, Splendor Forum, Jasola District Centre, New Delhi – 110025, India

103 Penang Road, #05–06/07, Visioncrest Commercial, Singapore 238467

Cambridge University Press & Assessment is a department of the University of Cambridge.

We share the University's mission to contribute to society through the pursuit of
education, learning and research at the highest international levels of excellence.

www.cambridge.org
Information on this title: www.cambridge.org/9781009040785

© Cambridge University Press & Assessment 2013, 2017

This publication is in copyright. Subject to statutory exception and to the provisions
of relevant collective licensing agreements, no reproduction of any part may take
place without the written permission of Cambridge University Press & Assessment.

First published 2013
Fifth edition 2017
Fifth edition update published 2021

20 19 18 17 16 15 14 13 12 11 10 9 8 7 6 5 4 3 2

Printed in Great Britain by CPI Group (UK) Ltd, Croydon CR0 4YY

A catalogue record for this publication is available from the British Library

ISBN	978-1-009-04052-5	Student's Book 3 with eBook
ISBN	978-1-009-04053-2	Student's Book 3A with eBook
ISBN	978-1-009-04054-9	Student's Book 3B with eBook
ISBN	978-1-009-04075-4	Student's Book 3 with Digital Pack
ISBN	978-1-009-04077-8	Student's Book 3A with Digital Pack
ISBN	978-1-009-04078-5	Student's Book 3B with Digital Pack
ISBN	978-1-316-62276-6	Workbook 3
ISBN	978-1-316-62277-3	Workbook 3A
ISBN	978-1-316-62279-7	Workbook 3B
ISBN	978-1-108-40711-3	Teacher's Edition 3
ISBN	978-1-316-62230-8	Class Audio 3
ISBN	978-1-009-04079-2	Full Contact 3 with Digital Pack
ISBN	978-1-009-04080-8	Full Contact 3A with Digital Pack
ISBN	978-1-009-04081-5	Full Contact 3B with Digital Pack
ISBN	978-1-108-40307-8	Presentation Plus 3

Additional resources for this publication at cambridgeone.org

Cambridge University Press & Assessment has no responsibility for the persistence
or accuracy of URLs for external or third-party internet websites referred to in this
publication, and does not guarantee that any content on such websites is, or will
remain, accurate or appropriate. Information regarding prices, travel timetables, and
other factual information given in this work is correct at the time of first printing but
Cambridge University Press & Assessment does not guarantee the accuracy of such
information thereafter.

Informed by teachers

Teachers from all over the world helped develop *Interchange Fifth Edition*. They looked at everything – from the color of the designs to the topics in the conversations – in order to make sure that this course will work in the classroom. We heard from 1,500 teachers in:

- Surveys
- Focus Groups
- In-Depth Reviews

We appreciate the help and input from everyone. In particular, we'd like to give the following people our special thanks:

Jader Franceschi, **Actúa Idiomas,** Bento Gonçalves, Rio Grande do Sul, Brazil

Juliana Dos Santos Voltan Costa, **Actus Idiomas,** São Paulo, Brazil

Ella Osorio, **Angelo State University,** San Angelo, TX, US

Mary Hunter, **Angelo State University,** San Angelo, TX, US

Mario César González, **Angloamericano de Monterrey, SC,** Monterrey, Mexico

Samantha Shipman, **Auburn High School,** Auburn, AL, US

Linda, **Bernick Language School,** Radford, VA, US

Dave Lowrance, **Bethesda University of California,** Yorba Linda, CA, US

Tajbakhsh Hosseini, **Bezmialem Vakif University,** Istanbul, Turkey

Dilek Gercek, **Bil English,** Izmir, Turkey

Erkan Kolat, **Biruni University, ELT,** Istanbul, Turkey

Nika Gutkowska, **Bluedata International,** New York, NY, US

Daniel Alcocer Gómez, **Cecati 92,** Guadalupe, Nuevo León, Mexico

Samantha Webb, **Central Middle School,** Milton-Freewater, OR, US

Verónica Salgado, **Centro Anglo Americano,** Cuernavaca, Mexico

Ana Rivadeneira Martínez and Georgia P. de Machuca, **Centro de Educación Continua – Universidad Politécnica del Ecuador,** Quito, Ecuador

Anderson Francisco Guimerães Maia, **Centro Cultural Brasil Estados Unidos,** Belém, Brazil

Rosana Mariano, **Centro Paula Souza,** São Paulo, Brazil

Carlos de la Paz Arroyo, Teresa Noemí Parra Alarcón, Gilberto Bastida Gaytan, Manuel Esquivel Román, and Rosa Cepeda Tapia, **Centro Universitario Angloamericano,** Cuernavaca, Morelos, Mexico

Antonio Almeida, **CETEC,** Morelos, Mexico

Cinthia Ferreira, **Cinthia Ferreira Languages Services,** Toronto, ON, Canada

Phil Thomas and Sérgio Sanchez, **CLS Canadian Language School,** São Paulo, Brazil

Celia Concannon, **Cochise College,** Nogales, AZ, US

Maria do Carmo Rocha and CAOP English team, **Colégio Arquidiocesano Ouro Preto – Unidade Cônego Paulo Dilascio,** Ouro Preto, Brazil

Kim Rodriguez, **College of Charleston North,** Charleston, SC, US

Jesús Leza Alvarado, **Coparmex English Institute,** Monterrey, Mexico

John Partain, **Cortazar,** Guanajuato, Mexico

Alexander Palencia Navas, **Cursos de Lenguas, Universidad del Atlántico,** Barranquilla, Colombia

Kenneth Johan Gerardo Steenhuisen Cera, Melfi Osvaldo Guzman Triana, and Carlos Alberto Algarín Jiminez, **Cursos de Lenguas Extranjeras Universidad del Atlantico,** Barranquilla, Colombia

Jane P Kerford, **East Los Angeles College,** Pasadena, CA, US

Daniela, **East Village,** Campinas, São Paulo, Brazil

Rosalva Camacho Orduño, **Easy English for Groups S.A. de C.V.,** Monterrey, Nuevo León, Mexico

Adonis Gimenez Fusetti, **Easy Way Idiomas,** Ibiúna, Brazil

Eileen Thompson, **Edison Community College,** Piqua, OH, US

Ahminne Handeri O.L Froede, **Englishouse escola de idiomas,** Teófilo Otoni, Brazil

Ana Luz Delgado-Izazola, **Escuela Nacional Preparatoria 5, UNAM,** Mexico City, Mexico

Nancy Alarcón Mendoza, **Facultad de Estudios Superiores Zaragoza, UNAM,** Mexico City, Mexico

Marcilio N. Barros, **Fast English USA,** Campinas, São Paulo, Brazil

Greta Douthat, **FCI Ashland,** Ashland, KY, US

Carlos Lizárraga González, **Grupo Educativo Anglo Americano, S.C.,** Mexico City, Mexico

Hugo Fernando Alcántar Valle, **Instituto Politécnico Nacional, Escuela Superior de Comercio y Administración- Unidad Santotomás, Celex Esca Santo Tomás,** Mexico City, Mexico

Sueli Nascimento, **Instituto Superior de Educação do Rio de Janeiro,** Rio de Janeiro, Brazil

Elsa F Monteverde, **International Academic Services,** Miami, FL, US

Laura Anand, **Irvine Adult School,** Irvine, CA, US

Prof. Marli T. Fernandes (principal) and Prof. Dr. Jefferson J. Fernandes (pedagogue), **Jefferson Idiomass,** São Paulo, Brazil

Herman Bartelen, **Kanda Gaigo Gakuin,** Tokyo, Japan

Cassia Silva, **Key Languages,** Key Biscayne, FL, US

Sister Mary Hope, **Kyoto Notre Dame Joshi Gakuin,** Kyoto, Japan

Nate Freedman, **LAL Language Centres,** Boston, MA, US

Richard Janzen, **Langley Secondary School,** Abbotsford, BC, Canada

Christina Abel Gabardo, **Language House,** Campo Largo, Brazil

Ivonne Castro, **Learn English International,** Cali, Colombia

Julio Cesar Maciel Rodrigues, **Liberty Centro de Línguas,** São Paulo, Brazil

Ann Gibson, **Maynard High School,** Maynard, MA, US

Martin Darling, **Meiji Gakuin Daigaku,** Tokyo, Japan

Dax Thomas, **Meiji Gakuin Daigaku,** Yokohama, Kanagawa, Japan

Derya Budak, **Mevlana University,** Konya, Turkey

B Sullivan, **Miami Valley Career Technical Center International Program,** Dayton, OH, US

Julio Velazquez, **Milo Language Center,** Weston, FL, US

Daiane Siqueira da Silva, Luiz Carlos Buontempo, Marlete Avelina de Oliveira Cunha, Marcos Paulo Segatti, Morgana Eveline de Oliveira, Nadia Lia Gino Alo, and Paul Hyde Budgen, **New Interchange-Escola de Idiomas,** São Paulo, Brazil

Patrícia França Furtado da Costa, Juiz de Fora, Brazil Patricia Servín

Chris Pollard, **North West Regional College SK,** North Battleford, SK, Canada

Olga Amy, **Notre Dame High School,** Red Deer, Canada

Amy Garrett, **Ouachita Baptist University,** Arkadelphia, AR, US

Mervin Curry, **Palm Beach State College,** Boca Raton, FL, US

Julie Barros, **Quality English Studio,** Guarulhos, São Paulo, Brazil

Teodoro González Saldaña and Jesús Monserrrta Mata Franco, **Race Idiomas,** Mexico City, Mexico

Autumn Westphal and Noga La`or, **Rennert International,** New York, NY, US

Antonio Gallo and Javy Palau, **Rigby Idiomas,** Monterrey, Mexico Tatiane Gabriela Sperb do Nascimento, **Right Way,** Igrejinha, Brazil

Mustafa Akgül, **Selahaddin Eyyubi Universitesi,** Diyarbakır, Turkey

James Drury M. Fonseca, **Senac Idiomas Fortaleza,** Fortaleza, Ceara, Brazil

Manoel Fialho S Neto, **Senac – PE,** Recife, Brazil

Jane Imber, **Small World,** Lawrence, KS, US

Tony Torres, **South Texas College,** McAllen, TX, US

Janet Rose, **Tennessee Foreign Language Institute,** College Grove, TN, US

Todd Enslen, **Tohoku University,** Sendai, Miyagi, Japan

Daniel Murray, **Torrance Adult School,** Torrance, CA, US

Juan Manuel Pulido Mendoza, **Universidad del Atlántico,** Barranquilla, Colombia

Juan Carlos Vargas Millán, **Universidad Libre Seccional Cali,** Cali (Valle del Cauca), Colombia

Carmen Cecilia Llanos Ospina, **Universidad Libre Seccional Cali,** Cali, Colombia

Jorge Noriega Zenteno, **Universidad Politécnica del Valle de México,** Estado de México, Mexico

Aimee Natasha Holguin S., **Universidad Politécnica del Valle de México UPVM,** Tultitlàn Estado de México, Mexico

Christian Selene Bernal Barraza, **UPVM Universidad Politécnica del Valle de México,** Ecatepec, Mexico

Lizeth Ramos Acosta, **Universidad Santiago de Cali,** Cali, Colombia

Silvana Dushku, **University of Illinois Champaign,** IL, US

Deirdre McMurtry, **University of Nebraska – Omaha,** Omaha, NE, US

Jason E Mower, **University of Utah,** Salt Lake City, UT, US

Paul Chugg, **Vanguard Taylor Language Institute,** Edmonton, Alberta, Canada

Henry Mulak, **Varsity Tutors,** Los Angeles, CA, US

Shirlei Strucker Calgaro and Hugo Guilherme Karrer, **VIP Centro de Idiomas,** Panambi, Rio Grande do Sul, Brazil

Eleanor Kelly, **Waseda Daigaku Extension Centre,** Tokyo, Japan

Sherry Ashworth, **Wichita State University,** Wichita, KS, US

Laine Bourdene, **William Carey University,** Hattiesburg, MS, US

Serap Aydın, Istanbul, Turkey

Liliana Covino, Guarulhos, Brazil

Yannuarys Jiménez, Barranquilla, Colombia

Juliana Morais Pazzini, Toronto, ON, Canada

Marlon Sanches, Montreal, Canada

Additional content contributed by Kenna Bourke, Inara Couto, Nic Harris, Greg Manin, Ashleigh Martinez, Laura McKenzie, Paul McIntyre, Clara Prado, Lynne Robertson, Mari Vargo, Theo Walker, and Maria Lucia Zaorob.

Classroom Language Student questions

Plan of Book 3B

Titles/Topics	Speaking	Grammar
UNIT 9 PAGES 58–63		
Getting things done Everyday services; recommendations; self-improvement	Talking about things you need to have done; asking for and giving advice or suggestions	Get or have something done; making suggestions with modals + verbs, gerunds, negative questions, and infinitives
UNIT 10 PAGES 64–69		
A matter of time Historic events and people; biography; the future	Talking about historic events; talking about things to be accomplished in the future	Referring to time in the past with adverbs and prepositions: *during, in, ago, from…to, for, since*; predicting the future with *will*, future continuous, and future perfect
PROGRESS CHECK PAGES 70–71		
UNIT 11 PAGES 72–77		
Rites of passage Milestones and turning points; behavior and personality; regrets	Describing milestones; describing turning points; describing regrets and hypothetical situations	Time clauses: *before, after, once, the moment, as soon as, until, by the time*; expressing regret with *should (not) have* + past participle; describing hypothetical situations with *if* clauses + past perfect and *would/could have* + past participle
UNIT 12 PAGES 78–83		
Keys to success Qualities for success; successful businesses; advertising	Describing qualities for success; giving reasons for success; interviewing for a job; talking about ads and slogans	Describing purpose with infinitive clauses and infinitive clauses with *for*; giving reasons with *because, since, because of, for, due to*, and *the reason*
PROGRESS CHECK PAGES 84–85		
UNIT 13 PAGES 86–91		
What might have been Pet peeves; unexplained events; reactions; complicated situations and advice	Drawing conclusions; offering explanations; describing hypothetical events; giving advice for complicated situations	Past modals for degrees of certainty: *must (not) have, may (not) have, might (not) have, could (not) have*; past modals for judgments and suggestions: *should (not) have, could (not) have, would (not) have*
UNIT 14 PAGES 92–97		
Creative careers Movies; media and entertainment professions; processes	Describing how something is done or made; describing careers in film, TV, publishing, gaming, and music	The passive to describe process with *is/are* + past participle and modal + *be* + past participle; defining and non-defining relative clauses
PROGRESS CHECK PAGES 98–99		
UNIT 15 PAGES 100–105		
A law must be passed! Recommendations; opinions; community issues; controversial topics	Giving opinions for and against controversial topics; offering a different opinion; agreeing and disagreeing	Giving recommendations and opinions with passive modals: *should be, ought to be, must be, has to be, has got to be*; tag questions for opinions
UNIT 16 PAGES 106–111		
Reaching your goals Challenges; accomplishments; goals; inspirational sayings	Giving opinions about inspirational sayings; talking about the past and the future	Accomplishments with the simple past and present perfect; goals with the future perfect and *would like to have* + past participle
PROGRESS CHECK PAGES 112–113		
GRAMMAR PLUS PAGES 140–151		

9 Getting things done

▸ Discuss professional services
▸ Make suggestions

1 SNAPSHOT

Small Business Directory

My account

Home | Advertise | Business reviews | Find a business | Quick search

Automotive
Auto repair

Car wash

Computers and Electronics
Computer repair and data recovery

Security systems repair

Personal Services and Care
Carpet cleaning

Home repairs

Home and Garden
Laundry and dry cleaning

Language tutoring

Why would someone need these services? Have you ever used any of them?
How do you choose a company or person to do any of these services?

2 PERSPECTIVES Get the job done!

▸ **A** Listen to an advertisement. Would you use a service like this? Why or why not?

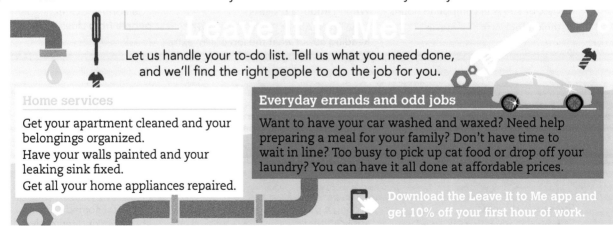

Leave It to Me!

Let us handle your to-do list. Tell us what you need done, and we'll find the right people to do the job for you.

Home services

Get your apartment cleaned and your belongings organized.
Have your walls painted and your leaking sink fixed.
Get all your home appliances repaired.

Everyday errands and odd jobs

Want to have your car washed and waxed? Need help preparing a meal for your family? Don't have time to wait in line? Too busy to pick up cat food or drop off your laundry? You can have it all done at affordable prices.

Download the Leave It to Me app and get 10% off your first hour of work.

B What services do you need or want? What questions would you ask before hiring a person to do these services for you?

3 GRAMMAR FOCUS

▶ Get or have something done

Use *get* or *have*, the object, and the past participle of the verb to describe a service performed for you by someone else.

Do something yourself	Get/have something done for you
I **clean** my house every week.	I **get** my house **cleaned** (by a cleaner) every week.
He **is painting** his bedroom.	He **is having** his bedroom **painted**.
They **fixed** the sink.	They **got** the sink **fixed**.
Did you **paint** your bedroom?	Did you **have** your bedroom **painted**?
Where can I **wash** my car?	Where can I **have** my car **washed**?

GRAMMAR PLUS *see page 140*

A Complete the sentences to express that the services are performed by someone else.

1. My parents didn't paint their house before they moved in. They _had it painted_. (have)
2. I didn't repair my own laptop. I _____ at the electronics store. (get)
3. Many people don't wash their cars. They _____. (have)
4. My bedroom carpet is very dirty, but I'm not cleaning it. I'm _____ next week. (get)
5. My brother isn't repairing his bike. He _____. (have)

B PAIR WORK Take turns describing the services in the pictures.

1. Jessica   2. Peter   3. Zoey   4. Tricia

"Jessica is having her nails done."

C PAIR WORK Tell your partner about three things you've had done for you recently. Ask and answer questions for more information.

4 PRONUNCIATION Sentence stress

▶ A Listen and practice. Notice that when the object becomes a pronoun (sentence B), it is no longer stressed.

A: Where can I have my car washed?   A: Where can I get my nails done?

B: You can have it washed at the auto shop.   B: You can get them done at a salon.

B GROUP WORK Ask questions about three things you want to have done. Pay attention to sentence stress. Other students give answers.

5 DISCUSSION On demand

PAIR WORK Are these services available in your city? For those that aren't, do you think they would be a good idea?

Can you . . . ?

get groceries delivered to your door
have a five-star meal cooked at your home by a chef
have your home organized by a professional organizer
have your portrait drawn by a street artist
get your pet vaccinated at home
get your blood pressure checked at a pharmacy
have your shoes shined on the street
get your car washed for less than $15
have a suit made in under 24 hours
have pizza delivered after midnight

A: Can you get groceries delivered to your door?
B: Sure! You can have it done by . . .

6 INTERCHANGE 9 Absolutely not!

What do parents and teenagers usually argue about? Go to
Interchange 9 on page 123.

7 WORD POWER Three-word phrasal verbs

A Match each phrasal verb in these sentences with its meaning.
Then compare with a partner.

Phrasal verbs
1. Polly has **broken up with** her
   boyfriend. _____
2. Lin **came up with** a great idea for
   a new app for meeting people. _____
3. My brother is **looking forward to** getting
   married. He really loves
   his fiancée. _____
4. I can't **keep up with** all the new
   technology. It changes so fast. _____
5. Luisa doesn't **get along with** her
   roommate. They argue over every
   little thing. _____
6. My doctor says I'm overweight. I should
   cut down on sweets. _____
7. I can't **put up with** the noise on my
   street! I'll have to move. _____
8. I don't like to **take care of** my own
   finances. I have an accountant manage
   my money. _____

Meanings
a. reduce the quantity of
b. end a romantic relationship with
c. continue to learn about
d. tolerate
e. be excited for
f. have a good relationship with
g. be responsible for
h. think of; develop

B PAIR WORK Take turns making sentences with each phrasal verb in part A.

8 CONVERSATION I can't carry a tune.

▶ **A** Listen and practice.

Emma: Are you going to Lina's party tonight?

Alice: No, I don't think so. I don't really feel up to it.

Emma: You haven't been going out much since you broke up with Carter.

Alice: I guess not. He's friends with all my friends, you know.

Emma: You need to meet new people. Have you thought about joining a running club? You love running.

Alice: I've thought about that, but they meet at 6 A.M. I'm not really a morning person.

Emma: Well . . . maybe you could take part in our singing group. I've made a lot of good friends there.

Alice: Um, I don't think so. Remember when we did karaoke? I can't carry a tune to save my life!

Emma: Yeah, I remember. . . . Well, I guess you'd better get used to waking up early. Just think of all the cute guys who go running in the park in the morning.

B CLASS ACTIVITY What are some other good ways to meet people?

9 GRAMMAR FOCUS

▶ **Making suggestions**

With modals + verbs
Maybe you could take part in a singing group.

With negative questions
Why don't you do some volunteer work?

With gerunds
What about joining a running club?
Have you thought about asking your friends to introduce you around?

With infinitives
One option is to join a club.
It might be a good idea to check out the cultural events at the university.

GRAMMAR PLUS *see page 140*

A Circle the correct answers. Then practice with a partner.

1. **A:** What can I do to keep up with all my assignments in college?
   B: Maybe / One option you could stay in on weeknights.

2. **A:** What can I do to get in shape?
   B: Why don't you / Have you thought about working out at the gym?

3. **A:** How can I save money?
   B: Why don't you / What about come up with a budget?

4. **A:** How can I learn to dance?
   B: Have you thought about / It might be a good idea to take dance classes.

5. **A:** How can I build self-confidence?
   B: What about / Why don't you participating in more social activities?

B GROUP WORK Take turns asking and answering the questions in part A. Answer with your own suggestions.

10 LISTENING Resolutions

▶ **A** Listen to a conversation between three friends on New Year's Eve. Check (✓) the resolution each person makes and write their friends' suggestions.

	New Year's resolutions		Suggestions
1. Edward	☐ get a better job	☐ start a project	
2. Selena	☐ have more energy	☐ go back to school	
3. Hannah	☐ fix her relationship problems	☐ spend more time on social media	

B GROUP WORK Decide on your own suggestion for each person. Then vote as a class on the best suggestions.

11 SPEAKING Breaking a habit

GROUP WORK Make three suggestions for how to break each of these bad habits. Then share your ideas with the class. Which ideas are the most creative?

How can I stop . . . ?

drinking too much soda

biting my nails

spending more money than I can afford

"One thing you could do is carry a bottle of water with you all the time. And why don't you . . . ?"

12 WRITING Sound advice

A Read the posts from a question and answer website. Choose one of the posts below and make a list of suggestions. Then write a reply.

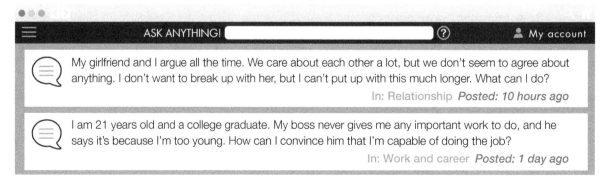

ASK ANYTHING!   ⊙   👤 My account

> My girlfriend and I argue all the time. We care about each other a lot, but we don't seem to agree about anything. I don't want to break up with her, but I can't put up with this much longer. What can I do?
>
> In: Relationship *Posted: 10 hours ago*

> I am 21 years old and a college graduate. My boss never gives me any important work to do, and he says it's because I'm too young. How can I convince him that I'm capable of doing the job?
>
> In: Work and career *Posted: 1 day ago*

B GROUP WORK Take turns reading your advice. Whose advice do you think will work? Why?

A Scan the article. Who is the article about? What idea did he have?

Improving the world

– one idea at a time

[1] Jack Andraka was 15 when he came up with an idea for a new way to test for pancreatic cancer. When Andraka was 14, a family friend died of the disease, and this affected him deeply. This kind of cancer is particularly lethal because there is no test you can have done to find it in the early stages. By the time standard tests determine you have the disease, it is often too late. Realizing that this was the case, Andraka decided to try to develop a test that might catch problems at the earliest stages.

[2] The road ahead looked difficult for Andraka. He was still a high school student, and he wanted to create something that no one else had done. But Andraka read endlessly about the disease, wrote a proposal for his idea, and sent it out to 200 cancer researchers. Only one professor, Dr. Anirban Maitra, responded positively. Dr. Maitra agreed to work with Andraka on his idea, giving him guidance and access to a laboratory.

[3] The next big reward for Andraka's perseverance was winning the grand prize at the Intel International Science and Engineering Fair. This prestigious award is given to young innovators who have developed a world-changing idea. Developing the test is likely to take many years, but Andraka hopes the test will eventually improve people's lives – and maybe save them.

[4] Jack Andraka is not alone as a young innovator. After all, there were 1,499 other contestants for the Intel award, and all of them had ground-breaking ideas. For Andraka, having a family that loves science and encourages creative thinking gave him an advantage. But the key for Andraka is that reading, research, and discovery are just plain fun – and the chance to improve the world around him in the process makes it even better.

B Read the article. Write the number of each paragraph next to its summary sentence.

_____ One doctor's help makes the unlikely become possible.

_____ A personal experience creates a groundbreaking idea.

_____ Family support and a passion for discovery can lead to great things.

_____ Although he won a big prize, there's plenty of work ahead.

C Choose the correct answers.

1. Pancreatic cancer is so serious because **there is no treatment / it is hard to diagnose early**.
2. Andraka was inspired to find a solution by **an upsetting experience / reading about a disease**.
3. The response to Andraka's proposal was **fairly positive / largely negative**.
4. Andraka's test for pancreatic cancer is **in use now / being developed now**.
5. Andraka's family helped him by **encouraging him / working on his idea**.

D GROUP WORK If you could come up with an idea to help humanity, what would it be?

A matter of time

▸ Discuss important past events
▸ Make predictions

1 SNAPSHOT

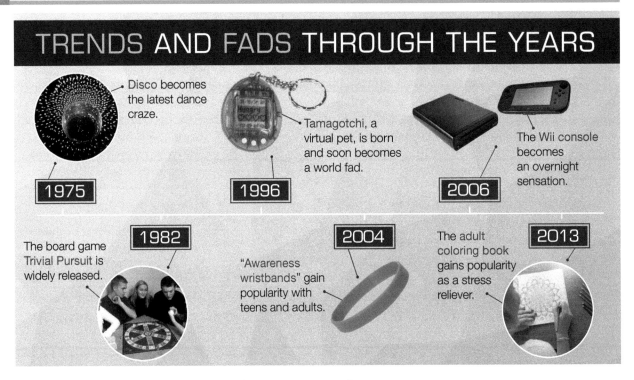

TRENDS AND FADS THROUGH THE YEARS

Disco becomes the latest dance craze.

1975

Tamagotchi, a virtual pet, is born and soon becomes a world fad.

1996

The Wii console becomes an overnight sensation.

2006

The board game Trivial Pursuit is widely released.

1982

"Awareness wristbands" gain popularity with teens and adults.

2004

The adult coloring book gains popularity as a stress reliever.

2013

Have any of these fads ever been popular in your country?
Can you think of other fads from the past or present?
Is there anything popular right now that you think is just a fad?

2 PERSPECTIVES Quiz show

A Read the questions from a quiz show. Do you know the answers? Check (✓) your guesses.

1. **When was the first home video game console released?**
   ☐ **a.** in 1967   ☐ **b.** in 1972   ☐ **c.** in 1981

2. **How long has Washington, D.C., been the capital of the United States?**
   ☐ **a.** since 1776   ☐ **b.** since 1783   ☐ **c.** since 1800

3. **How long were the Beatles together?**
   ☐ **a.** for 8 years   ☐ **b.** for 10 years   ☐ **c.** for 15 years

4. **When did World War I take place?**
   ☐ **a.** during the 1910s   ☐ **b.** during the 1920s   ☐ **c.** during the 1940s

▶ B Now listen and check your answers. What information is the most surprising?

GRAMMAR FOCUS

▶ **Referring to time in the past**

A point or period of time in the past

When was the first video game console released? How long were the Beatles together?
  During the 1970s. **In** the 1970s. Over 40 years **ago**.   **From** 1960 **to** 1970. **For** 10 years.

A period of time that continues into the present

How long has Washington, D.C. been the capital of the United States?
  Since 1800. **For** about 220 years.

GRAMMAR PLUS *see page 141*

A Complete the paragraphs with the **bold** words from the grammar box.
Then compare with a partner.

1. The Olympic Games originated in ancient
   Greece about 3,000 years _____. _____ the
   eighth century BCE _____ the fourth century CE,
   the games took place in Olympia. The first
   modern Olympics were held _____ 1896 in Athens,
   with male participants from 14 nations. Women
   have only competed in the Olympics _____ 1900.

2. Although no one knows for sure, it's likely that the
   Chinese invented ice cream about 4,000 years
   _____. It was probably brought to Italy _____
   the thirteenth century by Marco Polo, but the
   ice cream we enjoy today was probably created
   in Italy _____ the seventeenth century and spread
   through Europe _____ the eighteenth century.
   _____ that time, different flavors have been
   created, but vanilla is still America's favorite.

B GROUP WORK Write two true and two false statements about world events.
Then take turns reading your statements. Others give correct information for
the false statements.

A: The United Nations was founded about 50 years ago.
B: That's false. It was founded in 1945, after the end of World War II.

4 PRONUNCIATION Syllable stress

▶ **A** Listen and practice. Notice which syllable has the main stress in these four-
and five-syllable words. Notice the secondary stress.

● ◉ ● ●   ● ● ◉ ●   ● ● ◉ ●
identify   **disadvantage**   **communication**

_____   _____   _____

_____   _____   _____

appreciate
assassination
catastrophe
consideration
conversation
revolution

▶ **B** Listen to the words in the box. Which syllable has the main stress?
Write the words in the correct column in part A.

5 WORD POWER Historic events

A Match each word with the best example. Then compare with a partner.

1. achievement _____
2. assassination _____
3. discovery _____
4. election _____
5. epidemic _____
6. natural disaster _____
7. revolution _____
8. terrorist act _____

a. In 2015, an earthquake hit Nepal and killed over 8,000 people.
b. Fidel Castro established a communist government in Cuba in 1959.
c. In 2015, scientists confirmed the existence of water on Mars.
d. Since the early 1980s, HIV has infected more than 70 million people.
e. Barack Obama became the first African American US president in 2009.
f. John Lennon was killed by a fan on December 8, 1980.
g. In 2003, scientists completed the Human Genome Project.
h. Two men invaded and killed the journalists of the *Charlie Hebdo* newspaper in Paris in 2015.

B PAIR WORK Give another example for each kind of event in part A.

"The invention of writing was a very important achievement for humankind."

6 DISCUSSION A major impact

GROUP WORK Choose two or three historic events (an election, an epidemic, an achievement, etc.) that had an impact on your country. Discuss the questions.

What happened (or what was achieved)? When did it happen?
What was the immediate effect on your country? the world? your family?
Did it change things permanently? How is life different now?

"The recent economic crisis has had a major impact on our lives . . ."

7 WRITING A biography

A Find information about a person who has had a major influence on the world or your country. Answer these questions. Then write a biography.

What is this person famous for?
How and when did he or she become famous?
What are his or her important achievements?

MALALA YOUSAFZAI
Activist for Women and Children's Rights

Malala was born in 1997 in Pakistan where she spoke out for girls' right to education. When she was 15, she suffered an attack on her life and almost died. She was flown to England, recovered from her injuries, and continued her fight. When she was 17, she became the youngest winner of the Nobel Peace Prize . . .

B PAIR WORK Exchange biographies. What additional details can your partner add?

8 INTERCHANGE 10 History buff

Find out how good you are at history.
Student A, go to Interchange 10A on page 124; Student B, go to Interchange 10B on page 126.

CONVERSATION I'll be their first guest!

A Listen and practice.

Hazel: Would you want to spend a vacation in space?

Oscar: No, thanks. I'd rather go to the beach. Would you?

Hazel: Of course I would! I'd stay longer, too. Do you think we'll have colonies on Mars in 20 or 30 years?

Oscar: I don't know. Considering how fast we're destroying Earth, we won't be living here for much longer.

Hazel: I'm serious! You know, international space agencies are investing a lot of money in research to develop more powerful rockets.

Oscar: Well, I guess that within 50 years, we'll have set up a research center on Mars, but not a colony.

Hazel: You're probably right. But I'm sure some company will have built a resort on the moon by then. And I'll be their first guest!

B CLASS ACTIVITY Do you think Hazel and Oscar's predictions are correct?

10 GRAMMAR FOCUS

Predicting the future with *will*

Use *will* to predict future events or situations.

We **will spend** vacations in space. We **won't have** colonies on Mars.

Use future continuous to predict ongoing actions.

Human beings **will be living** on another planet. We **won't be living** here.

Use future perfect to predict actions that will be completed by a certain time.

Within 50 years, we **will have set up** a research center on Mars.

By 2050, a company **will have built** a resort on the moon.

GRAMMAR PLUS *see page 141*

A Complete these predictions with the correct verb forms. (More than one answer is possible.) Then compare with a partner.

1. Sometime in the future, buildings _____ (have) green walls and roof gardens to help retain carbon dioxide.

2. By the end of this century, half of the Amazon rain forest _____ (be) deforested.

3. In 50 years, the world population _____ (reach) 9 billion.

4. In the future, most of the population _____ (live) in cities.

5. Soon, computers _____ (become) more intelligent than humans.

6. In less than 20 years, scientists _____ (discover) a cure for cancer, but we _____ (suffer) from new diseases.

B GROUP WORK Discuss each prediction in part A. Do you agree or disagree?

A: Sometime in the future, buildings will have green walls and roof gardens to help retain carbon dioxide. What do you think?

B: Oh, I totally agree. That's also a good way to keep the temperature inside cooler in the summer.

C: I'm not so sure that will happen. Green walls are pretty expensive to maintain.

C CLASS ACTIVITY Discuss these questions.

1. What three recently developed technologies will have the greatest impact on our lives in the next 20 years?

2. What are the three most important changes that will have occurred on Earth by 2050?

3. Which three jobs will people *not* be doing in 50 years? Why?

11 LISTENING Not in our lifetime

A Listen to people discuss changes that will affect these topics in the future. Write down two changes for each topic.

	Future changes	
1. crime		
2. space travel		
3. environment		
4. energy		
5. money		

B PAIR WORK Which changes do you agree will happen? Which ones would most affect you? Why?

12 DISCUSSION Time will tell.

A Think about your dreams and goals for the future. Write down an idea for each category.

an activity you'd like to try   a city where you would like to live
an experience you'd like to have   a job you'd like to have
a skill you'd like to develop   a person you'd like to meet

B GROUP WORK Talk about these questions. Use your ideas from part A.

What do you think you'll be doing a year from now? five years from now?

Do you think you'll still be living in the same city? same country?

What are three things you think you'll have accomplished within the next 10 years?

What are three things you won't have done within the next 10 years?

In what ways do you think you'll have changed by the time you retire?

A: A year from now, I think I'll have a new hobby, like slacklining.

B: I'd like to try that, but I'm more interested in traveling.

C: Me too! I think in five years, I'll be living abroad.

13 READING

A Skim the article. Which sentence below could be another title for the article? Why?

Professionals Who Can Change the Future   An Unhappy View of the Future
Good Guesses About the Future

HOME   NEWS   ABOUT   POPULAR NOW

LOOKING INTO THE FUTURE

Futurists (sometimes called futurologists) are professionals who make predictions about the future of human society, the earth, and even the universe. They study the past and present in order to understand how things change and what factors can alter or interrupt these changes.

Since most people are curious about the future, futurists often try to picture how our lives will be different in a certain year. 2050 is a popular target since it is far enough away to require some speculation, but close enough that many of us will see the changes in our lifetime. Here are some of their predictions.

In the area of technology, computers will be nearly a billion times more powerful than they are today. That means that there will be almost no limit to what you can create, store, and display. Computers will also be small enough to implant in people's brains to improve memory, vision, or even to allow paralyzed people to move again. For those who love shopping or travel, a technology called "immersive telepresence" will allow us to actually feel like we are in two places at the same time, buying things in expensive foreign shops or visiting fascinating tourist destinations while sitting at home.

There will be many more people on earth – as many as 9.6 billion. This means that food production and housing will need to increase dramatically. People will live in *mushroom cities*, skyscrapers that house many people and use solar power and other eco-friendly technologies. Futurists also think that – thanks to advances in genetics – we will be close to finding cures for most human diseases. Some futurists even predict that wars and other conflicts will become less common as people learn that they have to get along in order to survive.

Of course, none of these predictions is a certainty. Even futurists can't know how epidemics, natural disasters, or climate change will alter our lives. Having some idea of what is in store for us, however, may help us to make the best choices for our own personal future.

B Read the article. Check (✓) the predictions futurists made about the year 2050.

1. ☐ Computers will be as powerful as they are today.
2. ☐ Tiny computers will help people with physical problems.
3. ☐ Travel will be faster than it is now.
4. ☐ People will be able to explore places without leaving home.
5. ☐ People will need less food.
6. ☐ Many people will live together in eco-friendly buildings.
7. ☐ People will not get sick anymore.
8. ☐ People will fight with each other over food and water.

C GROUP WORK Do you agree that the predictions in the article are likely? What changes would you like to see in the future?

SELF-ASSESSMENT

How well can you do these things? Check (✓) the boxes.

I can . . .	Very well	OK	A little
Discuss professional services (Ex. 1)	☐	☐	☐
Give advice and make suggestions (Ex. 2)	☐	☐	☐
Understand and discuss historic events (Ex. 3)	☐	☐	☐
Make predictions about the future (Ex. 4)	☐	☐	☐

1 DISCUSSION Professional services

GROUP WORK Take turns asking questions about these services. When someone answers "yes," find out why and when the service was performed, and who performed it.

have a piece of clothing tailor-made for you
get your carpet cleaned
have your home redecorated or remodeled
get something translated
have your cell phone repaired

A: Have any of you ever had a piece of clothing tailor-made for you?
B: Yes, I have. I had a suit tailor-made when I got married.
C: Really? Why didn't you buy one in a store? . . .

2 ROLE PLAY Advice needed

Student A: Choose one of these problems. Decide on the details of the problem.
Then tell your partner about it and get some advice.

I want to move to my own place, but I don't make enough money.
I never have time to do any of the things I enjoy doing. I'm always busy with . . .
I have a job interview in English, and I'm feeling nervous about it.
My in-laws are coming to dinner, but I can't cook at all.

Student B: Your partner tells you about a problem.
Ask questions about it.
Then consider the situation and offer
two pieces of advice.

Change roles and choose another situation.

useful expressions

Have you thought about . . . ?
It might be a good idea to . . .
Maybe you could . . .
Why don't you . . . ?

3 LISTENING Important world events

▶ **A** Listen to people discuss the questions. Write the correct answers.

1. What date did people first land on the moon? _____
2. When was the first World Cup? _____
3. When was the Chernobyl disaster? _____
4. How long did it take to build the *Titanic*? _____
5. When did the Indian Ocean tsunami occur? _____

B PAIR WORK Which of these events would you like to learn more about? Why?

C GROUP WORK Write three more questions about historic events. (Make sure you know the answers.) Then take turns asking your questions. Who has the most correct answers?

4 SURVEY What will happen?

A CLASS ACTIVITY How many of your classmates will have done these things in the next 5 years? Write down the number of "yes" and "no" answers. When someone answers "yes," ask follow-up questions.

	"Yes" answers	"No" answers
1. get a (new) job		
2. develop a new skill		
3. move to a new home		
4. learn another language		
5. travel abroad		
6. get a college or master's degree		

A: Five years from now, will you have moved to a new home?
B: Yes, I think I will be living in a new place.
A: Where do you think you'll be living?
B: I'd like to live in a bigger place. Our current apartment is too small.
A: Really? Would you rather live in a house or an apartment?

B GROUP WORK Tally the results of the survey as a group. Then take turns telling the class any additional information you found out.

"Most people think they will have moved to a new home. Only three people think they'll be living at their current address. One person thinks she'll be living in a big house in the suburbs, and . . . "

WHAT'S NEXT?

Look at your Self-assessment again. Do you need to review anything?

Rites of passage

▶ Discuss life events and milestones
▶ Describe regrets and hypothetical situations

1 SNAPSHOT

UNFORGETTABLE FIRSTS

Some moments that matter

- ☐ first sleepover
- ☐ losing your first tooth
- ☐ first day at school
- ☐ first pet
- ☐ first swim in the ocean
- ☐ first crush

- ☐ first trip with friends
- ☐ high school graduation
- ☐ first paycheck
- ☐ getting your driver's license
- ☐ entering college
- ☐ first heartbreak

a sleepover

Which of these first experiences were important for you?
Check (✓) them.
How did you feel when you had these experiences?
What other first experiences have you had that you will never forget?

2 CONVERSATION I was so immature.

▶ **A** Listen and practice.

Jim: Congratulations, graduate! What's next for my favorite nephew?

Luke: I'm your *only* nephew, Uncle Jim!

Jim: But you're still my favorite! Anyway, what *are* your plans?

Luke: I'm looking for a job, so I can make some money before I go to college.

Jim: Ah! After *I* graduated, I went to Alaska to work as a fisherman. It was a tough job, but it helped me grow up.

Luke: How do you mean?

Jim: Until I started working, I'd never had any important responsibilities. I was so immature. But once I moved away from home, I learned to take care of myself.

Luke: So you became independent.

Jim: Yeah, but not for very long, actually. After two months, I moved back home . . . and got a job at your grandfather's store.

Luke: Hey, I think my search just ended. I'm going to talk to Grandpa about a job.

▶ **B** Listen to the rest of the conversation. What was an important turning point for Jim? for Luke?

GRAMMAR FOCUS

▶ **Time clauses**

Before I graduated from high school, I had never worked.

After I graduated, I went to Alaska to work as a fisherman.

Once I moved away from home, I learned to take care of myself.

The moment I moved away from home, I felt like a different person.

As soon as I got my own bank account, I started to be more responsible.

Until I moved to Alaska, I had never been away from home.

By the time I went to college, I had already lived away from home.

GRAMMAR PLUS *see page 142*

A Match the clauses in column A with appropriate information in column B. Then compare with a partner.

A	B
1. Until I went to college, _____	**a.** I learned the importance of teamwork.
2. Before I became a parent, _____	**b.** I understood why you shouldn't text and drive.
3. Once I joined a sports team, _____	**c.** I realized that I wasn't a child anymore.
4. The moment I had a car accident, _____	**d.** I learned that love can hurt!
5. As soon as I got my first paycheck, _____	**e.** I had never taken school very seriously.
6. By the time I was 15, _____	**f.** I began to understand the value of money.
7. After I began a relationship, _____	**g.** I had never cooked a real meal.
8. Until I left home, _____	**h.** I had never worried about the future.

B Which of the clauses in column A can you relate to your life? Add your own information to those clauses. Then compare with a partner.

"Until I left home, I had never bought my own clothes."

C GROUP WORK What do you think people learn from these events? Write sentences using time clauses in the present. Then take turns reading and talking about them.

1. moving in with roommates
2. buying your own home
3. having a pet
4. getting a credit card
5. getting your first paycheck
6. getting your driver's license
7. getting married
8. becoming a parent

1.   "Once you move in with roommates, you have to learn to work together."

4 LISTENING Turning points

▶ **A** Listen to three people describe important events in their lives.
Complete the chart.

	Turning point	How it affected him or her
1. Nari		
2. Anthony		
3. Karina		

▶ **B** Listen again. What do these three people have in common?

C PAIR WORK What has been a turning point in your life?
Discuss with a partner.

5 SPEAKING Milestones

A PAIR WORK In your country, how old are people when these
things typically happen?

get a first job   graduate from college
get a driver's license   get married
move out of their parents' home   retire

B GROUP WORK Choose three milestones. What do
you think life is like before and after each one?
Join another pair and discuss.

"Before you get a job, you depend on your family
for everything. The moment you get your first
paycheck, you . . ."

6 WORD POWER Personal characteristics

A PAIR WORK At what age do you think people possess these traits?
Check (✓) one or more ages for each trait.

	In their teens	In their 20s	In their 30s	In their 40s	In their 60s
ambitious	☐	☐	☐	☐	☐
argumentative	☐	☐	☐	☐	☐
carefree	☐	☐	☐	☐	☐
dependable	☐	☐	☐	☐	☐
naive	☐	☐	☐	☐	☐
pragmatic	☐	☐	☐	☐	☐
rebellious	☐	☐	☐	☐	☐
sophisticated	☐	☐	☐	☐	☐
wise	☐	☐	☐	☐	☐

B GROUP WORK Use the words in part A to describe people you know.
"My mother is dependable. I can always count on her when I need help."

7 PERSPECTIVES That was a mistake.

A Listen to two recent college graduates talk about their regrets.
Do you have any similar regrets?

1. I should have done an internship while I was in college.

2. If I'd been more ambitious in college, I could have learned to speak another language.

3. If I hadn't been so irresponsible, I could have gotten better grades.

4. I shouldn't have taken out a student loan to pay for college.

5. If I'd listened to my professors, I would have taken some additional courses.

6. If I hadn't wasted so much money last year, I would have saved enough to start graduate school.

B GROUP WORK What advice would you give to these recent grads?

8 GRAMMAR FOCUS

Expressing regret and describing hypothetical situations

Use *should have* + the past participle to express regret.
I should have done an internship while I was in college.
I shouldn't have taken out a student loan.

Use *would have* + the past participle to express probable outcomes in hypothetical situations.
Use *could have* + the past participle to express possible outcomes.
If **I'd listened** to my professors, I **would have taken** additional courses.
If I **hadn't been** so irresponsible, I **could have gotten** better grades.

GRAMMAR PLUS *see page 142*

A For each statement, write a sentence expressing regret. Then talk with a partner about which statements are true for you.

1. I didn't play any sports when I was younger.
2. I was carefree with money when I was a teenager.
3. I didn't stay in touch with my school friends after I graduated.
4. I was naive when I first started working.
5. I didn't study hard in school.

> 1. I should have played sports when I was a teenager.

B Match the clauses in column A with appropriate information in column B.

A
1. If I hadn't gone to so many parties, _____
2. If I'd been more careful, _____
3. If I'd been wiser, _____
4. If I'd listened to my financial advisor, _____
5. If I hadn't been so rebellious, _____

B
a. I would have been nicer to my parents.
b. I wouldn't have borrowed money for a new car.
c. I would have done better in school.
d. I wouldn't have lost all my documents.
e. I wouldn't have argued with my boss.

C Add your own information to the clauses in column A. Then compare in groups.

9 INTERCHANGE 11 Good choices, bad choices

Imagine if things were different. Go to Interchange 11 on page 125.

10 PRONUNCIATION Reduction of *have* and *been*

A Listen and practice. Notice how **have** and **been** are reduced in these sentences.

I should **have been** less selfish when I was younger.
If I'd **been** more ambitious, I could **have** gotten a promotion.

B PAIR WORK Complete these sentences and practice them. Pay attention to
the reduced forms of **have** and **been**.

I should have been . . . when I was younger. If I'd been more . . ., I could have . . .
I should have been . . . in school. If I'd been less . . ., I would have . . .

11 LISTENING My biggest regret

A Listen to a conversation between three friends about regrets. Write two regrets
that each person has.

	Regrets	
1. Ariana		
2. Ray		
3. Kira		

B Listen again. Which friend feels differently about regrets? How does he or she feel?

C PAIR WORK Do you agree with the attitude about regrets in part B? Why or why not?

12 WRITING An apology

A Think about something you regret doing that you want to apologize for.
Consider the questions below. Then write a message of apology.

What did you do? What were the consequences?
Is there any way you can undo those consequences?

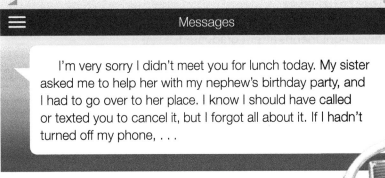

100% 🔋
≡ Messages 🔍

I'm very sorry I didn't meet you for lunch today. My sister
asked me to help her with my nephew's birthday party, and
I had to go over to her place. I know I should have called
or texted you to cancel it, but I forgot all about it. If I hadn't
turned off my phone, . . .

B PAIR WORK Read your partner's message.
Talk about what you would have done if
you'd had a similar regret.

13 READING

A Skim the advice column. What is Paul's problem? What does he ask Stella?

STELLA'S ANSWERS

| HOME | ABOUT | ADVICE | ASK STELLA | COMMUNITY | FOLLOW STELLA |

Dear Stella,

I have a problem, and I'm not sure what to do about it. I was studying with my friend Karl, and he let me use his laptop for a minute to look something up. He had been busy typing an essay, so I opened the document again when I was done. But somehow I hit the wrong button, and I deleted the document. All of his work was gone. It was a total accident, and I did say, "Sorry," just so he wouldn't yell at me. But he got really angry and accused me of doing it on purpose. Now Karl is acting really cold towards me, and I can tell he's still angry. It really wasn't my fault, but I still feel bad. Should I apologize anyway just to make him feel better?

Paul in Philadelphia

Dear Paul,

When you've done something that hurt a friend, even by accident, it can be really uncomfortable. You obviously feel bad about deleting Karl's essay, and you didn't mean for it to happen. Unfortunately, it sounds like Karl has a pretty *short fuse*. Sure, if you'd apologized better at the time, and if you had offered to help him recover his work, it might have smoothed things over. After being accused of *sabotage*, however, I understand why you didn't apologize again.

What should you do now? First, ask yourself if an apology is necessary. If you don't feel you did anything wrong, it wouldn't mean very much. An apology has to be sincere and *heartfelt* to be effective. Second, if someone stops treating you like a friend because you made a mistake – which is a form of emotional *blackmail* – they probably won't believe your apology anyway. Third, a two-way discussion is often more effective than an apology. I think you need to sit down with Karl, tell him how badly you feel, avoid making excuses or trying to blame him, and get on with your friendship. If he still won't *forgive* you after that, maybe he's not such a great friend after all.

B Read the advice column. Find the words in *italics* in the text. Match the definitions to the words.

1. *short fuse* _____
2. *sabotage* _____
3. *heartfelt* _____
4. *blackmail* _____
5. *forgive* _____

a. act of demanding something from someone in exchange for a benefit
b. quick or violent temper
c. decide not to be angry at someone
d. act of destroying something to get an advantage
e. very sincere

C Check (✓) True, False, or Not given for each statement.

	True	False	Not given
1. The two boys are best friends from childhood.	☐	☐	☐
2. Paul mistakenly deleted some of Karl's work.	☐	☐	☐
3. Karl reacted very calmly at the time.	☐	☐	☐
4. Stella thinks Paul could have improved the situation at the time.	☐	☐	☐
5. Stella believes that both friends need to apologize.	☐	☐	☐
6. Stella thinks even an insincere apology is helpful.	☐	☐	☐
7. Karl's behavior shows that he is not very forgiving.	☐	☐	☐
8. Stella says that Paul and Karl's friendship is over.	☐	☐	☐

D PAIR WORK Do you agree with the advice Stella gave Paul? If not, what advice would you give him?

Keys to success

▶ Give personal views and describe qualities for success
▶ Give reasons

1 SNAPSHOT

HOW SOME MAJOR COMPANIES GOT THEIR NAMES

Nike The company got its name from the ancient Greek goddess of victory.

Google Google comes from *googol*, which is the math term for the number 1 followed by 100 zeros.

Facebook The name was taken from the term for a list with students' names and photos found at American universities.

Samsung In Korean, *sam* means "three" and *sung* means "star," so the name means "three stars." It represents the idea that the company should be everlasting, like stars in the sky.

Skype The original concept for the name was Sky-Peer-to-Peer, which became Skyper, and then Skype.

Häagen-Dazs The name of the American ice cream brand was invented to sound Danish and traditional, but it has no meaning in any language.

Pepsi The soft drink got its name from the word *dyspepsia*, which means indigestion, because its inventor believed it helped treat an upset stomach.

Which of these brands exist in your country? Are they successful?
Do you know the origin of the names of other companies or brands?

2 PERSPECTIVES Business strategies

▶ **A** Listen to the survey. What makes a business successful? Number the choices from 1 (most important) to 3 (least important).

What makes a business successful?

1. **In order for an app to succeed, it has to be:**
   ☐ easy to use   ☐ inexpensive   ☐ original

2. **To attract talented professionals, a company should offer:**
   ☐ competitive salaries   ☐ flexible working schedules   ☐ a good career plan

3. **For a small company to be profitable, it should have:**
   ☐ a good marketing plan   ☐ a great product   ☐ excellent professionals

4. **To build a successful start-up, it's important to:**
   ☐ have a great product   ☐ have a clear business plan   ☐ control costs

5. **In order to finance a new business, it's a good idea to:**
   ☐ try a crowd-funding platform   ☐ get a bank loan   ☐ borrow money from family

6. **For people to work from home, they need to have:**
   ☐ self-discipline   ☐ a separate working space   ☐ a daily schedule

B GROUP WORK Compare your answers. Do you agree on the most important success factors?

3 PRONUNCIATION Reduced words

A Listen and practice. Notice how certain words are reduced in conversation.

In order **før ä** hotel **tø** be successful, it needs **tø** have friendly service **änd** reasonable prices.
Før än entrepreneur **tø** be successful, they have **tø** invest in **ä** good marketing campaign.

B PAIR WORK Take turns reading the sentences in Exercise 2 aloud. Use your first choice to complete each sentence. Pay attention to reduced words.

4 GRAMMAR FOCUS

Describing purpose

Infinitive clauses

To attract talented professionals,	a company should offer competitive salaries.
(In order) to finance a new business,	it's a good idea to get a bank loan.

Infinitive clauses with *for*

For a small company **to be** profitable,	it should have a good marketing plan.
(In order) for an app to succeed,	it has to be easy to use.

GRAMMAR PLUS *see page 143*

A Match each goal with a suggestion. Then practice the sentences with a partner. (More than one answer is possible.)

Goals

1. To run a popular convenience store, _____
2. In order to run a profitable clothing boutique, _____
3. To establish a successful language school, _____
4. In order for a health club to succeed, _____
5. For a restaurant to attract more customers, _____

Suggestions

a. it has to offer friendly service.
b. it's a good idea to know the competition.
c. you need to choose the right location.
d. you have to train your staff well.
e. it's important to understand your customers' needs.

B PAIR WORK Give another suggestion for each goal in part A.

C GROUP WORK What kind of business would you like to have? Talk to your classmates and get suggestions on how to make your business successful.

A: I think I'd like to set up a coffee shop.
B: For a coffee shop to succeed, it's important to choose a good location.
C: And in order to attract customers, you have to offer some tasty desserts, too.

5 WORD POWER Qualities for success

A PAIR WORK What qualities are important for success?
Rank them from 1 to 5.

A personal trainer	A politician	A news website
☐ athletic	☐ clever	☐ affordable
☐ passionate	☐ charming	☐ attractive
☐ industrious	☐ knowledgeable	☐ entertaining
☐ muscular	☐ persuasive	☐ informative
☐ experienced	☐ tough	☐ well written

B GROUP WORK Add one more adjective to each list.

"For a personal trainer to be successful, he or she needs to be . . ."

6 ROLE PLAY The job is yours!

Student A:

Interview two people for one of these jobs. What
qualities do they need for success? Decide who is
more qualified for the job.

Students B and C:

You are applying for the same job. What are your
best qualities? Convince the interviewer that you
are more qualified for the job.

sales associate at a trendy boutique   public relations specialist   tour guide

A: To be a good sales associate, you need to be persuasive. Are you?
B: Oh, yes. I'm very good at convincing people. And I'm industrious.
C: I've worked at other stores before, so I'm experienced. And I'm fashionable, too.

7 CONVERSATION It's always packed.

A Listen and practice.

Kyle: What's your favorite club, Lori?
Lori: The Firefly. They have fabulous music, and it's never
crowded, so it's easy to get in.
Kyle: That's funny. There's always a long wait outside my
favorite club. I like it because it's always packed.
Lori: Why do you think it's so popular?
Kyle: Well, it just opened a few months ago, everything is
brand-new and modern, and lots of trendy people
go there. It's called the Dizzy Lizard.
Lori: Oh, right! I hear the reason people go there is
just to be seen.
Kyle: Exactly! Do you want to go some night?
Lori: I thought you'd never ask!

B CLASS ACTIVITY What are some popular places in your
city? Do you ever go to any of these places? Why or
why not?

8 GRAMMAR FOCUS

▶ Giving reasons

The Firefly is famous **for** its fantastic music.

I like the Dizzy Lizard **because** it's always packed.

Since it's always so packed, there's a long wait outside the club.

It's popular **because of** the trendy people.

Due to the crowds, the Dizzy Lizard is difficult to get into.

The reason (**that/why**) people go there **is** just to be seen.

GRAMMAR PLUS *see page 143*

A Complete the paragraphs with *because, since, because of, for, due to,* and *the reason*. Then compare with a partner. (More than one answer is possible.)

1. Apple is considered one of the most innovative companies in the world. The company is known _____ introducing original products, but it's also admired _____ its ability to predict what the market will need in the future. _____ Apple has been so successful is that it has become a symbol of status and high-end technology.

2. McDonald's is popular worldwide _____ customers know what to expect when they eat there. Whether you're in Florida or in France, your Big Mac is the same. The company is also known _____ its ability to adapt to different markets. _____ the company adjusts some items to local tastes, you can eat a pineapple pie in Thailand or a shrimp burger in Japan.

B **PAIR WORK** Match the situations with the reasons for success. Compare ideas with a partner. Then give two more reasons for each success.

Situation

1. FedEx is famous _____
2. Samsung is a successful company _____
3. Online stores are becoming very popular _____
4. Netflix has expanded quickly _____
5. People buy Levi's jeans _____
6. Many people like Amazon _____
7. Nike is known _____
8. People everywhere drink Coca-Cola _____

Reason

a. because of its ability to attract new customers.
b. for its fast and reliable service.
c. for its innovative athletic wear.
d. for its wide selection of products.
e. since prices are generally more affordable.
f. due to its high investment in research.
g. since it's advertised worldwide.
h. because they appeal to people of different ages and lifestyles.

A: FedEx is famous for its fast and reliable service.

B: I think another reason why FedEx is famous is . . .

C **GROUP WORK** What are some successful companies in your country? Why are they successful?

9 LISTENING What have you got to lose?

▶ **A** Listen to radio commercials for three different businesses.
What are two special features of each place?

	Fitness For Life	Beauty To Go	Like-New Repair Services
1.			
2.			

▶ **B** Listen again. Complete the slogan for each business.

1. "Fitness For Life, where _____."
2. "Beauty To Go. When and where you want, beauty _____."
3. "Like-New Repair Services. Don't let your phone _____."

C GROUP WORK Which business do you think would be the most
successful in your city? Why?

10 INTERCHANGE 12 Advertising taglines

How well do you know the slogans companies use for their products?
Go to Interchange 12 on page 127.

11 DISCUSSION Ads and commercials

GROUP WORK Discuss these questions.

When you watch TV, do you pay attention to the commercials? Why or why not?
When you're online, do you click on any ads that you see?
   What ads attract your attention?
What are some effective commercials or ads you remember?
   What made them effective?
What is the funniest commercial you've ever seen? the worst? the most shocking?
Which celebrities have been in commercials or ads?
   Has this affected your opinion of the product?
   Has it affected your opinion of the celebrity?

12 WRITING A commercial

A Choose one of your favorite products. Read the
questions and make notes about the best way to sell
it. Then write a one-minute TV or online commercial.

What's good or unique about the product?
Why would someone want to buy or use it?
Can you think of a clever name or slogan?

B GROUP WORK Take turns presenting your commercials.
What is good about each one? Can you give any
suggestions to improve them?

Do you want a car that is dependable and economical? Do you need more space for your family? The new Genius SUV has it all. Genius offers the latest safety technologies and . . .

A Scan the article. What does "sticky" mean in the advertising world?

BRAIN INVASION:
WHY WE CAN'T FORGET SOME ADS

Advertisements: They're all over our social media pages; they arrive as text messages; they interrupt our favorite shows; and they bombard us in the streets. In order to survive the constant barrage of advertising, we learn to ignore most of what we see. But what is it that makes certain ads "sticky"? In other words, why do we remember some ads while managing to completely forget others?

According to advertising experts, an ad needs three key elements to make it unforgettable. In the first place, it needs to be clear and simple. TV commercials usually last about 30 seconds, so a complicated or confusing presentation will not do the job. For an ad to be "sticky," it has to be obvious enough that we can pick up the message in a split second.

More importantly, ads should appeal to our senses and emotions. When we really feel something, it tends to stick in our brains much longer than if we simply understand it. This is the reason why so much advertising depends on emotional music and images of family, romance, or success that relate directly to our own hopes and dreams.

One more element necessary to make an ad successful is surprise. When we see something out of the ordinary, it makes us take notice whether we want to or not. A talking animal, a beautifully dressed model diving into a swimming pool, a car zooming through an ever-changing landscape – these are the types of things that grab our attention.

But do "sticky" ads actually make us buy the products? That's another story. Sometimes the most memorable ads make people laugh or mention them to their friends, but they don't actually convince people to buy anything. Still, after watching a "sticky" ad, we usually remember the name of the company it promotes. And in a world with so many brands and products, that is almost as important as sales.

B Read the article. Check (✓) the three things that make an ad memorable.

- [ ] an uncomplicated concept
- [ ] a puzzle or mystery
- [ ] a short time span
- [ ] a sensual or emotional appeal
- [ ] a familiar scene or situation
- [ ] something unexpected or strange

C Read these descriptions of two ads. According to the article, are these "sticky" ads? Explain why.

A family of four is having breakfast together, and they're all looking tired. The father pours each of them a glass of "Super Juice," and as they all drink it, they are transformed into costumed superheroes. As they leave, the mother says, "Ready to save the world, team?"

A young couple are in a luxurious car; the woman is driving. They are driving quickly through lush countryside. They glance at other and smile. A voiceover says: "The Eternity: a car that feels like home."

D **PAIR WORK** Describe an advertisement that has stuck in your mind. Why do you think you remember it? Has it influenced what you buy in any way?

Units 11–12 Progress check

SELF-ASSESSMENT

How well can you do these things? Check (✓) the boxes.

I can . . .	Very well	OK	A little
Describe important life events and their consequences (Ex. 1)	☐	☐	☐
Describe and explain regrets about the past (Ex. 2)	☐	☐	☐
Describe hypothetical situations in the past (Ex. 2)	☐	☐	☐
Understand and give reasons for success (Ex. 3, 4)	☐	☐	☐
Give reasons (Ex. 4)	☐	☐	☐

1 SPEAKING Important events

A What are two important events for each of these age groups?
Complete the chart.

Children	Teenagers	People in their 20s	People in their 40s

B GROUP WORK Talk about the events. Why is each event
important? What do people learn from each event?

A: Learning to drive is an important event for teenagers.
B: Why is learning to drive an important milestone?
A: Once they learn to drive, . . .

useful expressions	
after	once
as soon as	before
the moment	until
by the time	

2 GAME Regrets

A Write three regrets you have about the past.

1.   I wish I hadn't argued with my boss.

B GROUP WORK What if the situations were different?
Take turns. One student expresses a regret. The next
student adds a hypothetical result, and so on, for as long
as you can.

A: I shouldn't have argued with my boss.
B: If you hadn't argued with your boss, she wouldn't
have fired you.
C: If she hadn't fired you, you could have . . .

3 LISTENING The road to success

A Listen to a career coach discuss some factors necessary to work for yourself. Write down the three factors that you hear.

	Factor	Why is it important?
1.		
2.		
3.		

B Listen again. In your own words, write why each factor is important.

C PAIR WORK If you could work for yourself, what would you do? Why?

4 DISCUSSION Effective strategies

A PAIR WORK Choose two businesses and discuss what they need to be successful. Then write three sentences describing the most important factors.

☐ a convenience store   ☐ a dance club   ☐ a juice bar
☐ a gourmet supermarket   ☐ a beach hotel   ☐ a used clothing store

> In order for a convenience store to be successful, it has to be open 24 hours.

B GROUP WORK Join another pair. Share your ideas. Do they agree?

A: We think in order for a convenience store to be successful, it has to be open 24 hours.

B: Really? But many convenience stores close at midnight.

C GROUP WORK Now choose a popular business that you know about. What are the reasons for its success?

"I think Mark's Comics is successful because their comic books are affordable and they don't mind if people hang out there and read."

useful expressions

It's successful because (of) . . .
It's popular due to . . .
The reason it's successful is . . .
It's become popular since . . .
It's famous for . . .

WHAT'S NEXT?

Look at your Self-assessment again. Do you need to review anything?

What might have been

▶ Suggest explanations and reasons
▶ Give opinions and advice about past situations

1 SNAPSHOT

PET PEEVES

IT DRIVES ME CRAZY WHEN . . .

- people push too close to me on the subway.
- someone borrows my things without asking.
- people keep interrupting me.
- a couple starts arguing in public.
- people don't pay for their share at a restaurant.
- a friend criticizes another friend.
- someone is late for no reason.
- people chew with their mouths open.
- a friend constantly asks me for favors.
- someone cuts in line in front of me.

Which of the pet peeves do you have about people you know? Which one is the worst?
What other pet peeves do you have?
Do you do any of these things? When and why?

2 CONVERSATION He might have gone out.

▶ **A** Listen and practice.

Chris: Didn't Tyler ask us to come at 7:30?

Ava: Yes, and it's almost 8:00 now. Why don't we ring the bell again? He must not have heard it.

Chris: That's impossible. We've been ringing the bell for more than 10 minutes.

Ava: He must have fallen asleep. You know Tyler has been working so hard on his new project.

Chris: Or he might have forgotten about our dinner and just gone out.

Ava: No, he couldn't have forgotten. I just talked to him about it this morning. Besides, the lights are on. He could have had an emergency. He might not have had time to call us.

Chris: Yeah, maybe. I'll call him and find out.

Ava: And?

Chris: He's not answering. . . . Now *I'm* getting worried.

▶ **B** Listen to the rest of the conversation. What happened?

3 PRONUNCIATION Reduction in past modals

A Listen and practice. Notice how **have** is reduced in these sentences.

He may ~~have~~ fallen asleep.   She might ~~have~~ gone out.

B Listen and practice. Notice that **not** is not contracted or reduced in these sentences.

He might **not** have had time to call us.   She must **not** have heard the doorbell.

4 GRAMMAR FOCUS

Past modals for degrees of certainty

It's almost certain.	It's possible.
He **must have fallen** asleep.	He **may/might have gone** out.
He **must not have heard** the doorbell.	He **may/might not have had** time to call us.
It's not possible.	He **could have had** an emergency.
He **couldn't have forgotten** about it.	

GRAMMAR PLUS *see page 144*

A Read each situation and choose the best explanation. Then practice with a partner.
(Pay attention to the reduced forms in past modals.)

Situation

1. Marcia seems very relaxed. _____
2. Claire is packing her things. _____
3. Jeff got a bad grade on his test. _____
4. Rodrigo looks very tired today. _____
5. Julia didn't talk to her friends in the cafeteria. _____
6. Ahmed got a call and looked worried. _____

Explanation

a. She must have gotten fired.
b. He might have worked late last night.
c. She may have just come back from vacation.
d. He couldn't have heard good news.
e. He might not have studied very hard.
f. She must not have seen them.

B PAIR WORK Suggest different explanations for each situation in part A.

5 LISTENING What could have happened?

A GROUP WORK Look at the pictures. What do you think happened?
Offer an explanation for each event.

B Listen to the explanations for the two events in part A and take notes.
What *did* happen? How similar were your explanations?

6 SPEAKING What's your guess?

A PAIR WORK What do you think were the reasons for these events? Suggest two different explanations for each.

1. The bride didn't show up for her wedding. She sent a bunch of flowers to the groom with a note: "Thank you."
2. A man arrived at the airport with a suitcase and saw his brother. He grabbed a cab and went back home.
3. It was a hot, sunny day. A man arrived home. He was soaking wet.

B GROUP WORK Each student thinks of two situations like the ones in part A. Others suggest explanations.

A: A man went around town and bought all the copies of the latest issue of a specific magazine.

B: Well, the magazine might have had an article about him.

7 INTERCHANGE 13 Think of the possibilities!

What's your best explanation for some unusual events? Go to Interchange 13 on page 128.

8 PERSPECTIVES I'm going nuts!

A Listen to a person complaining about her family members. Check (✓) the response you think is best for each problem.

Last night, my sister borrowed my car without asking. She did call me a couple of times, but I was in a meeting and couldn't answer the phone. We had a big fight, and now we're not speaking.

☐ She shouldn't have used your car without permission, no matter what.
☐ You could have been more understanding. After all, she tried to call you first.

My nephew is so inconsiderate. He called me at 3:00 in the morning to talk about his problems with his best friend, and I had to get up very early to work. I was really mad.

☐ You could have told him that you had to get up early the next day.
☐ Your nephew is always doing that. You shouldn't have answered his call.

My brother came over for the weekend with his wife and three kids. They made such a mess of the apartment! I'll never invite them over again.

☐ I would have asked them to help clean up the place.
☐ I wouldn't have invited them to spend the weekend. Having overnight guests can be really stressful.

B Do you talk about pet peeves with your friends? Do they give you advice?

9 GRAMMAR FOCUS

▶ Past modals for judgments and suggestions

Judging past actions	Suggesting alternative past actions
You **should have asked** your sister to help.	You **could have told** her that you had to get up early.
He **shouldn't have used** your car.	I **would have asked** them to help clean up the place.
	I **wouldn't have invited** them to spend the weekend.

GRAMMAR PLUS *see page 144*

A Complete the conversations using past modals with the verbs given. Then practice with a partner.

1. **A:** My boss asked me to help her choose a gift for her husband, and I ended up spending all day at the mall.

   B: You _____ (make up) an excuse not to help her. She _____ (not ask) for such a personal favor in the first place.

2. **A:** I lent my sister-in-law some money a year ago, and she never paid it back.

   B: She _____ (pay) it back already! Well, I _____ (not lend) money to her anyway. I never lend money to relatives.

3. **A:** Austin invited me out to dinner, but when the check came, he said he was broke!

   B: I _____ (not pay) for him. I _____ (tell) him to wash the dishes. He _____ (not invite) you if he didn't have enough money.

4. **A:** I can't believe my cousin came over and stayed until 1:00 in the morning!

   B: He _____ (not stay) so late. You _____ (start) yawning. Maybe he would have gotten the hint!

B PAIR WORK Think of another suggestion or comment for each situation above.

10 WORD POWER Reactions

A Helena's boyfriend forgot their anniversary. How does she react? Match each reaction with the best example.

Reaction	Example
1. an assumption _____	**a.** "Sometimes you're so selfish."
2. a criticism _____	**b.** "You could take me out to dinner."
3. a demand _____	**c.** "You must have wanted to break up with me."
4. an excuse _____	**d.** "I bet you went out with your friends."
5. a prediction _____	**e.** "Now you'll have to get me a really nice gift."
6. a suggestion _____	**f.** "I know you've been busy lately. It just slipped your mind."
7. a suspicion _____	**g.** "If you ever forget another important date, I'll never talk to you again."
8. a warning _____	**h.** "You'll probably forget my birthday, too!"

B GROUP WORK Imagine that someone was late for class, or choose another situation. Give an example of each reaction in the list above.

What might have been **89**

11 LISTENING What should they have done?

▶ **A** Listen to descriptions of three situations. What would have been the best thing to do in each situation? Check (✓) the best suggestion.

1. ☐ Simon should have kept the ring for himself.
   ☐ He should have called the police.
   ☐ He did the right thing.

2. ☐ Jana shouldn't have mentioned her last job at all in her application.
   ☐ She should have been honest in her application and admitted she made a mistake.
   ☐ She did the right thing.

3. ☐ Martin should have reported what his boss did as soon as he found out.
   ☐ He should have withdrawn more money and blamed it on his boss.
   ☐ He did the right thing.

B PAIR WORK What would you have done in each situation in part A?

12 DISCUSSION How would you have reacted?

GROUP WORK Read each situation. Say what the person could have or should have done, and what you would have done.

> " It was my friend's birthday, and he had invited a few close friends out to celebrate. I forgot all about it, so I called him the next day and pretended I'd had to take my mother to the hospital. " – Warren

> " My sister got a new haircut, and I thought it looked a little dated. I didn't want to hurt her feelings, so I told her I liked it. " – Sonia

> " I didn't have any money to buy my cousin a birthday present, so I gave her something I had received previously as a gift. My brother told my cousin about my regifting, and now she's mad at me. " – Chase

> " I went to my in-laws' house for dinner last night. My husband thinks his mother is a great cook, but the food was awful! I didn't know what else to do, so I ate it. " – Fay

A: Warren should have told his friend the truth.
B: I agree. He could have taken his friend out to make up for it.
C: I think I would have . . .

13 WRITING A tricky problem

A Think of a complicated situation from your own experience. Write a paragraph describing the situation, but don't explain how you resolved it.

> I have a close friend who doesn't get along with my other friends. He's a nice guy, friendly and funny, but every time we all go out, he makes a fuss over how much everyone should pay. Last week, my friends were going to dinner, and he wanted to come along. I didn't want to hurt his feelings . . .

B PAIR WORK Exchange papers. Write a short paragraph about how you would have resolved your partner's situation.

C PAIR WORK Read your partner's resolution to your situation. Tell your partner how you resolved it. Whose resolution was better?

A Skim the article. What do the two unexplained events have in common?

Messages from Outer Space, or a Leaking Pipe?

Home | Sciencenews | Technology | Articles | Blog | Community

Even though we know so much about the world around us, unexplained events still take place. Read about these two events. What do you think may have happened?

Since 2008, people around the world have been reporting a mysterious sound that seems to come from the sky. Some people say it sounds like trumpets playing. Others say it is like sound effects from sci-fi movies. The phenomenon has caused both fear and fascination, and many people have been looking for explanations. One popular idea is that the sound is an announcement of the end of the world, and another suggests that it's the sound of spaceships. But there may be a more scientific explanation. It involves flares from the sun and energy from the center of the earth. Which explanation do you think might be right?

Of course, there are some strange events that still baffle both the general public and experts. Take the high-pitched noise that has been driving people crazy in Forest Grove, Oregon. To some people, it sounds like a giant flute being played very badly, and to others, it sounds like a train slowing down or truck brakes squealing. The sound is coming from under the street, but gas, water, and sewer inspectors have said there is nothing wrong down there. One resident was so sure it was a serious gas leak that he was ready to flee. However, experts say that a leak would make a different sound, and people would definitely smell gas. How would you explain this mysterious and annoying event?

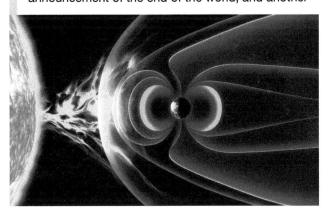

B Read the article. Then answer the questions.

1. To what two things have people compared the first sound?
2. What non-scientific explanations have been offered?
3. What sort of sound are people in Forest Grove hearing?
4. What explanation has been proven untrue?
5. If there had been a gas leak, what would be different?

C Which of these statements are facts? Which are opinions? Check (✓) Fact or Opinion.

	Fact	Opinion
1. Science has not explained everything that happens.	☐	☐
2. Some sounds mean the end of the world is coming.	☐	☐
3. The first sound is caused by energy from planets.	☐	☐
4. The sound in Forest Grove is very annoying.	☐	☐
5. The Forest Grove sound comes from under the street.	☐	☐
6. Gas lines and other systems in Forest Grove have no problems.	☐	☐
7. No local problems can explain the Forest Grove noise.	☐	☐

D PAIR WORK Which explanations of the events in the article do you think are the most likely? least likely? Can you think of any other possible explanations?

14 Creative careers

▸ Describe steps in a process
▸ Discuss jobs in entertainment and the media

1 SNAPSHOT

MILESTONES IN CONTEMPORARY CINEMATOGRAPHY

THE FIRST . . .

- movie with **Dolby Digital** sound. – *Batman Returns* (1992)
- **computer-animated** feature film. – *Toy Story* (1995)
- major movie **shot entirely in digital video.** – *Star Wars Episode II: Attack of the Clones* (2002)
- computer-animated **motion-captured** film. – *The Polar Express* (2004)
- movie to be **released simultaneously** in theaters, on DVD, and on the Internet. – *EMR* (2005)
- **film directed by a woman** to win the Oscar for Best Picture. – *The Hurt Locker* (2008)
- full-length feature film **shot on a phone.** – *Olive* (2011)
- major movie **filmed at 48 frames per second**, instead of the standard 24 fps. – *The Hobbit: An Unexpected Journey* (2012)

Have you seen any of these movies? Did you enjoy them?
What's the most popular movie playing right now? Have you seen it? Do you plan to?
Are there many movies made in your country? Name a few of your favorites.

2 CONVERSATION I have more control.

▶ **A** Listen and practice.

Clara: Thanks for coming to the film festival! Directing this film was amazing, and I'm happy to answer your questions about it.

Diego: Yes, hi. What is it like to direct an animated movie? Is it different from live action?

Clara: Well, for one thing, I have a lot more control. There are no actors to argue with me!

Diego: I guess not! But how do you direct cartoon characters?

Clara: Well, after a screenplay is chosen, many drawings of the characters are presented to me . . .

Diego: And you get to choose which ones to use?

Clara: Even better: I can change them if I want. The characters have to be drawn just right – like I see them in my mind.

Diego: So you decide a lot about the characters early on.

Clara: Definitely. By the time the voice actors are picked, the characters feel like old friends!

▶ **B** Listen to the rest of the conversation. Who helps Clara choose the voice actors?

3 GRAMMAR FOCUS

The passive to describe process

Is/are + past participle	Modal + be + past participle
A screenplay **is chosen**.	The characters **have to be drawn** just right.
Many drawings **are presented**.	The drawings **might be changed** 10 times.

GRAMMAR PLUS see page 145

A The sentences below describe how an animated movie is made. First, complete the sentences using the passive. Then compare with a partner.

Storyboard and animation steps

1. First, storyboards _____ (draw) by story artists. For some movies, over 200,000 storyboards might _____ (draw).

2. Next, the storyboards need to _____ (place) in order.

3. After the storyboarding process _____ (complete), technical directors must _____ (hire).

4. Then, the scenes and characters have to _____ (create) on the computer by the technical directors.

5. Finally, movement _____ (add) to the scenes by animators. In addition, the scenes _____ (populate) with background characters.

Voice-over steps

6. First, temporary "scratch" voices _____ (record). Sometimes scratch voices are so good that they _____ (not replace).

7. Later, professional actors _____ (hire) to record the character voices. For some movies, studios hire famous actors so their names can _____ (use) as a marketing tool.

8. The lines _____ (rehearse) and the same line _____ (record) in different ways.

9. Finally, the best recording _____ (choose) for the final movie.

B PAIR WORK What are some steps that happen after the animated movie is complete? Discuss with a partner.

"After all that, the movie is sent to theaters."

4 LISTENING It was too predictable.

A Listen to Casey and Grant talk about things that often happen in movies. Number the parts of a movie in the order they are mentioned.

	Movie example
☐ A new plan is put into action.	Luke planned to destroy the Death Star.
☐ A problem is presented.	
☐ Something bad happens, and all hope is lost.	
☐ The main character is introduced.	
☐ The bad guy is defeated.	

B Listen again. For each movie part above, write an example from the movies the friends discuss.

5 SPEAKING Tutorials

A PAIR WORK What do you think is required to make a short movie? Put the pictures in order and describe the steps. More than one order may be possible. Use the vocabulary to help you.

☐ add titles and credits

☐ rehearse the lines

☐ shoot the movie

☐ find a location

☐ edit the movie

1 write the script

A: Making a short movie requires many steps. First, the script needs to be written.
B: Right! And after that, a location must be found.
A: I agree. Then . . .

B PAIR WORK Choose one of these topics. Come up with as many steps as you can.

preparing a school party   organizing a fundraising campaign   developing a mobile app
organizing a trip abroad   planning a wedding   putting on a school musical

C GROUP WORK Share your information from part B with another pair.

6 WRITING Describing a process

A Write about one of the topics from Exercise 5, part B or use your own idea. Describe the different steps in the process.

> Developing a mobile app requires a lot of work. First, the objective of the app must be defined. Then, a prototype should be built. After that, the prototype can be tested by potential users or friends. Then a developer needs to be hired, and . . .

B PAIR WORK Read your partner's description. Can you think of any more steps?

7 WORD POWER Creative jobs

A What kind of jobs are these? Complete the chart with the compound nouns.
(More than one answer is possible.)

band manager	game animator	songwriter	talk show host
club DJ	gameplay programmer	storyboard artist	quality assurance analyst
editorial director	news photographer	stunt person	web content manager

Film/TV jobs	Publishing jobs	Gaming jobs	Music jobs

B GROUP WORK Choose four jobs from part A. Describe each job.

"A band manager negotiates contracts for artists and helps promote their careers."

8 PERSPECTIVES Career questions

A Listen to the career questions that people have. How would you answer them?

I have a degree in journalism, and I'm an amateur photographer. I'm considering a career as a news photographer who covers conflicts around the world. Do you think that's too dangerous?

Videographers like me, who shoot weddings and other social events, often work evenings and weekends. I want to have a nine-to-five job, so I'm looking for a job with a major studio. Is that a good move?

I love movies and I love action, so I'm thinking of becoming a stunt person – you know, the person who takes the place of an actor in dangerous scenes. What do you think?

A talk show host, who interviews artists, politicians, and celebrities, gets to meet lots of people. I love to meet new people. Do you think that would be a good job for me?

B PAIR WORK Which of these careers do you think would be the most interesting? Why?

9 PRONUNCIATION Review of stress in compound nouns

A Listen and practice. Notice how the first word in a compound noun usually receives greater stress.

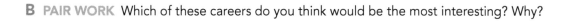

band manager   talk show host   game animator   news photographer   stunt person

B Practice the sentences in Exercise 8. Pay attention to the word stress in the compound nouns.

> **Defining and non-defining relative clauses**
>
> Defining relative clauses are used to identify people.
>
> I want to become a photographer.
> I want to cover conflicts. → I want to become a photographer **who/that covers conflicts**.
>
> Non-defining relative clauses give further information about people.
>
> Videographers shoot weddings and social events. They work evenings and weekends. → Videographers, **who shoot weddings and social events**, work evenings and weekends.
>
> GRAMMAR PLUS *see page 145*

A Do these sentences contain defining (**D**) or non-defining (**ND**) clauses? Write **D** or **ND**. Add commas to the non-defining clauses. Then compare with a partner.

1. The art editor who creates the look of a magazine should make it attractive. _____

2. A game programmer is the person who writes the computer code that runs and controls a game. _____

3. The extras are the people who appear in the background scenes. _____

4. The producer who is responsible for the budget is the big boss in an animation studio. _____

B Add the non-defining relative clauses in parentheses to the sentences.

1. A game designer works closely with the programmers. (who creates new games)

   _____

2. A lead vocalist is the main voice on stage. (who may also be a songwriter)

   _____

3. A news reporter collects information about news and events. (who should be impartial)

   _____

4. A photo editor selects the photos that go into magazines. (who is responsible for the quality and content of images)

   _____

C Write three sentences with relative clauses about jobs you know. Compare with a partner.

11 INTERCHANGE 14 Celebrities

Can you guess who the celebrities are? Go to Interchange 14 on page 129.

12 READING

A Scan the title and first paragraph of the article. Who do you think it was written for? Why?

Home | News | Entertainment | Articles | Blog | Community

THE TRUTH ABOUT BEING A FILM EXTRA
by Anna Murphy

When people discover that I work as a film and TV extra, they always ask me the same questions: *Is it easy to get work? Isn't it boring? Do you get to meet famous actors? Does it pay well?* My answers are pretty standard as well: yes, sometimes, once in a while, and . . . kind of. The life of an extra is both more interesting and more boring than you might imagine.

Extras, who play the people in crowds, on streets, or in the background of indoor scenes, can come from all walks of life. Unlike many extras, I'm a trained actor. I do get real speaking roles, but work can be hard to come by if you're not an in-demand star. I'm registered with an agency that deals exclusively with extras, so I get calls all the time. The agency explains who I'll be – someone in a crowd, a member of a jury, a clerk – and tells me where to go. Call time is usually bright and early, so I try to get to bed at a reasonable hour.

Sometimes being an extra is a "hurry up and wait" job. In my first extra role, I was one of a group of office workers who come out of a building just as a car explodes in the street. We waited for hours for the scene to be shot, and then went in and out of the building about fifty times, trying to act horrified by a nonexistent explosion. Then we had lunch, changed clothes, and spent the afternoon as customers in a department store.

It may sound like I don't enjoy the work, but I do. Being part of the background in a convincing way is challenging, and being on a film or TV set is always fascinating. A lot of famous actors don't even notice the extras, but the ones who do make the job a lot of fun for everyone. As for the money, it's nothing compared to what the big actors make, but it pretty much pays the bills. And, as a bonus, I've beaten my high scores on all my phone games, thanks to all the time I spend sitting around, waiting for something to happen.

B Read the article. Underline a sentence in the article that answers each question below.

  1. What training has the writer had?

  2. How does she get work as an extra?

  3. What was her first role as an extra?

  4. What unexpected advantage of the work does she mention?

C Find words or phrases in the article that mean the same as the following.

  1. have very different jobs and life experiences _____

  2. wanted or needed by many people _____

  3. first thing in the morning _____

  4. imaginary _____

  5. difficult _____

D PAIR WORK What job would you most like to have on a film or TV show? Why?

Units 13–14 Progress check

SELF-ASSESSMENT

How well can you do these things? Check (✓) the boxes.

I can . . .	Very well	OK	A little
Speculate about past events (Ex. 1)	☐	☐	☐
Give opinions and advice about past events (Ex. 2)	☐	☐	☐
Describe steps in processes (Ex. 3)	☐	☐	☐
Use relative clauses to give information about people (Ex. 4)	☐	☐	☐

1 LISTENING Something's not right.

A Listen to three conversations. Where do you think each conversation takes place? What do you think might have happened? Take notes.

	Location	What might've happened	What could've happened next
1.			
2.			
3.			

B PAIR WORK Decide what happened with your partner. Then decide what could have happened next in each situation. Complete the chart.

2 DISCUSSION Bad moves

A PAIR WORK React to these situations. First, make a judgment or suggestion using a past modal. Then add another statement using the reaction in parentheses.

1. Samantha didn't get to work on time today. (a suggestion)
2. Pat took a vacation, and now he doesn't have money for rent. (a warning)
3. Jim didn't study for the test, but he got all the answers correct. (a suspicion)
4. Nick was driving too fast, and the police stopped him. (an excuse)
5. Carl spent the night playing his favorite game online. (a prediction)

"Samantha should have left home earlier. She could have set an alarm."

B GROUP WORK Join another pair and compare your comments. Who has the most interesting reaction to each situation?

3 GAME Step by step

A **GROUP WORK** Look at these topics. Set a time limit. Talk with your group and write as many steps as you can between the first and last parts of each process.

making a grilled cheese sandwich

organizing a party

First, the bread has to be sliced.

_____
_____
_____
_____

Finally, the sandwich is served on a plate.

First, the guests have to be chosen.

_____
_____
_____
_____

Finally, the guests are welcomed.

B **CLASS ACTIVITY** Compare your answers. Which group has the most steps?

4 SPEAKING Your social circle

A Complete these statements about people in your life.

My best friend is a person who _____.
My neighbor, who _____, always _____.
My mother is someone that _____.
My teacher, who _____, is _____.
_____ is a _____ who
_____.

B **PAIR WORK** Compare your answers. Ask two follow-up questions about each of your partner's statements.

A: My best friend is a person who always listens to me when I have a problem.
B: Does she give you good advice?

WHAT'S NEXT?

Look at your Self-assessment again. Do you need to review anything?

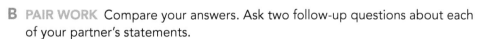

15 A law must be passed!

▸ Make recommendations about social issues
▸ Give opinions about laws and social issues

1 SNAPSHOT

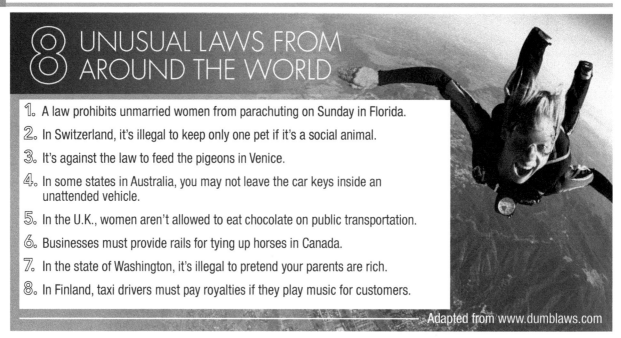

8 UNUSUAL LAWS FROM AROUND THE WORLD

1. A law prohibits unmarried women from parachuting on Sunday in Florida.
2. In Switzerland, it's illegal to keep only one pet if it's a social animal.
3. It's against the law to feed the pigeons in Venice.
4. In some states in Australia, you may not leave the car keys inside an unattended vehicle.
5. In the U.K., women aren't allowed to eat chocolate on public transportation.
6. Businesses must provide rails for tying up horses in Canada.
7. In the state of Washington, it's illegal to pretend your parents are rich.
8. In Finland, taxi drivers must pay royalties if they play music for customers.

Adapted from www.dumblaws.com

Which of these laws would you like to have in your city or country? Why?
Can you think of reasons for these laws?
Do you know of any other unusual laws?

2 PERSPECTIVES Rules and regulations

▶ **A** Listen to people make recommendations at a city council meeting. Would you agree with these proposals if they were made in your community? Check (✓) your opinion.

CITY OF BRISTOL

MEETING NOTES

	STRONGLY AGREE	SOMEWHAT AGREE	DISAGREE
1. Clubs should be required to install soundproof walls.	☐	☐	☐
2. Riding a bike on the sidewalk mustn't be permitted.	☐	☐	☐
3. Pet owners shouldn't be allowed to walk dogs without a leash.	☐	☐	☐
4. Something has got to be done about littering.	☐	☐	☐
5. A law must be passed to control the pollution from vehicles.	☐	☐	☐
6. Children ought to be required to wear a helmet when riding a bike.	☐	☐	☐
7. Schools should only be permitted to serve organic food.	☐	☐	☐

B GROUP WORK Compare your opinions. Try to get your classmates to agree with you.

3 GRAMMAR FOCUS

GRAMMAR PLUS see page 146

Giving recommendations and opinions

When you think something is a good idea

Clubs **should be required** to install soundproof walls.

Pet owners **shouldn't be allowed** to walk dogs without a leash.

People **ought (not) to be required** to wear a helmet when riding a bike.

When you think something is absolutely necessary

A law **must be passed** to control the pollution from vehicles.

Riding a bike on the sidewalk **mustn't be permitted**.

A rule **has to be made** to require bike lanes on city streets.

Something **has got to be done** to stop littering.

A Complete the sentences positively or negatively. Choose a modal that shows how strongly you feel about these issues.

1. Young people _____ (permit) to vote before age 21.
2. Laws _____ (pass) to protect people's online privacy.
3. People _____ (allow) to use offensive language in social media.
4. Governments _____ (require) to provide health care to all their citizens.
5. Children _____ (allow) to play violent video games.
6. Scientists _____ (permit) to use animals for research.
7. The sale of fur products _____ (prohibit).
8. Something _____ (do) to stop the pollution of rivers and oceans.

B GROUP WORK Compare your statements. Do you agree with one another? If not, why not?

A: Young people shouldn't be permitted to vote before age 21. They're not prepared.

B: You may have a point, but they could be better informed.

C: Maybe, but in my opinion, . . .

4 DISCUSSION Controversial topics

A GROUP WORK Think of three reasons for, and three reasons against, each idea below. Then discuss your views. As a group, form an opinion about each idea.

requiring employers to offer workers 12 weeks of parental leave

paying teachers less when their students fail

banning private cars from the downtown areas of big cities

A: What do you think about requiring employers to offer workers 12 weeks of parental leave?

B: I think it's a good idea. Parents should be allowed to stay with their babies . . .

offering a different opinion

That sounds interesting, but I think . . .

That's not a bad idea. On the other hand, I feel . . .

You may have a point. However, I think . . .

B CLASS ACTIVITY Share your group's opinions and reasons. Who has the most persuasive reasons for and against each position?

5 LISTENING Something has got to be done!

A Listen to people discuss annoying situations. Number the situations they describe in the correct order from 1 to 3. (There are three extra situations.)

- [ ] using the phone on speaker in public places
- [ ] using a cell phone on a plane
- [ ] posting selfies on social media
- [ ] taking selfies in crowded places
- [ ] not having signs about cell phones in public places
- [ ] texting in a movie theater

B Listen again. What solutions do they suggest for each situation?

1. _____
2. _____
3. _____

C GROUP WORK Do you agree or disagree with the solutions? What do you think should be done about each problem?

6 INTERCHANGE 15 On the wrong side of the law

What if you could make the rules? Go to Interchange 15 on page 130.

7 WORD POWER Community issues

A PAIR WORK Which of these issues are problems in your community? Check (✓) the appropriate boxes.

- [ ] bullying
- [ ] homelessness
- [ ] inadequate health care
- [ ] irregular trash collection
- [ ] lack of affordable child care
- [ ] noise pollution
- [ ] overcrowded classrooms
- [ ] stray animals
- [ ] street crime
- [ ] vandalism

B GROUP WORK Join another pair of students. Which three problems concern your group the most? What should or can be done about them?

vandalism

8 CONVERSATION It's not easy, is it?

▶ **A** Listen and practice.

Mara: I need to find a new apartment. I can't stand the noise from all those bars and clubs in my neighborhood anymore.

Ted: I can imagine. But it isn't easy to find a nice apartment in a quiet neighborhood, is it?

Mara: No, it's not! And my rent is already sky-high. I'm having a hard time making ends meet.

Ted: I know. Everything is really expensive nowadays, isn't it?

Mara: It sure is. You know, I'm looking for child care for my baby, but I just can't find anything affordable in the area.

Ted: The city should provide free child care to working families.

Mara: I think so, too. But unfortunately, the mayor doesn't.

▶ **B** Listen to the rest of the conversation. What is Ted concerned about?

9 GRAMMAR FOCUS

▶ **Tag questions for opinions**

Affirmative statement + negative tag	Negative statement + affirmative tag
Everything is really expensive nowadays, **isn't it**?	It isn't easy to find a nice apartment, **is it**?
There are lots of clubs around, **aren't there**?	There aren't any noise pollution laws, **are there**?
Mara likes her apartment, **doesn't she**?	Her neighbors don't make much noise, **do they**?
The city should provide child care, **shouldn't it**?	You can't sleep because of the noise, **can you**?

GRAMMAR PLUS *see page 146*

A Add tag questions to these statements. Then compare with a partner.

1. There aren't enough shelters for the homeless, . . . ?
2. Vandalism makes a neighborhood very unpleasant, . . . ?
3. In overcrowded classrooms, teachers can't give enough attention to students, . . . ?
4. School bullying is a major problem in most schools, . . . ?
5. There are more street crimes in big cities than in small towns, . . . ?
6. The government should provide adequate health care to everyone, . . . ?
7. The city doesn't do enough for stray animals, . . . ?
8. It isn't easy to save money these days, . . . ?

B What are some things you feel strongly about in your school or city? Write six statements with tag questions.

C GROUP WORK Take turns reading your statements. Other students respond by giving their opinions.

A: Public transportation isn't adequate, is it?

B: No, it isn't. There should be more bus lines.

C: On the other hand, the subway system is very efficient . . .

10 PRONUNCIATION Intonation in tag questions

A Listen and practice. Use falling intonation in tag questions when
you are giving an opinion and expect the other person to agree.

Noise pollution is a serious problem in our city, isn't it?

Governments should offer child care to all working families, shouldn't they?

B PAIR WORK Take turns reading the statements with tag questions
from Exercise 9, part A. Give your own opinions when responding.

11 LISTENING Let's face it.

A Listen to people give their opinions about issues in the news.
What issues are they talking about?

	Issue	Opinions for	Opinions against
1.			
2.			

B Listen again. Write the different opinions that you hear.

C GROUP WORK What do you think about the issues in part A? Give your own opinions.

12 WRITING There ought to be a law.

A Think about a local problem that needs
to be solved, and write a persuasive essay
suggesting a new law to help solve it. Be
creative! Use these questions to help you.

What is the problem, and how does it affect
your community?
What can be done to help solve it?
Who might disagree with you, and how will
you convince him or her that your law is a
good idea?

> The water crisis affects people all over the world. I think
> cities should be required to recycle their water. Also,
> people shouldn't be permitted to use clean drinking water
> to wash their cars and water their gardens. If people
> used recycled water, . . .

B GROUP WORK Try to convince your classmates to pass your new law. Then vote on it.

A Look at the title and the picture. What do you think plagiarism is?

● ● ● ‹ ›

| HOME | NEWS | ARTICLES | COMMUNITY |

THAT'S PLAGIARISM?

POSTED AUGUST 21

If a teacher or your boss called you aside and said that he or she suspected you of plagiarism, how would you react? You'd probably be honestly confused. Nowadays, there are so many sources of information available that you can copy from with a single click. Many people don't even realize that they're committing plagiarism. Whether it's intentional or not, using someone else's information is stealing, and stealing is definitely a big deal.

The confusion about ownership comes from the fact that articles, photos, blogs, and social media posts are so easy to access – and just as easy to copy. When you see the same article on various websites, it's fairly natural to assume that it's public property. If a resource like Wikipedia offers material that can be critiqued and changed by its readers, that must be free for the taking, right? But that simply is not the case. Everything that has been written, drawn, photographed, or recorded, and released to the public, belongs to someone. Even your friends' comments on your social media page belong to them, not to you.

To avoid plagiarism, here are a few basic points to keep in mind. When writing a paper, if you get ideas or wording from someone else's writing, you must include the name of the writer or the source. If you find a few articles that you want to use, and you think taking a few points from each article and combining them makes the content yours, it's just not the case. This kind of "masked" plagiarism is very easy to spot, and it will get you into trouble. But really, just asking yourself a simple question should be enough: "Are all of these words my own?" If the answer is yes, you're in the clear.

In the end, the best approach is to write down the source for any material you quote from directly, and to assume that if it's public, it isn't yours. Plagiarism is a serious problem and can have serious consequences – even if it's totally accidental. Besides, putting ideas into your own words can make you a better writer, and a better thinker as well.

B Read the article. Then answer the questions.

1. What is the author's main purpose in writing the piece?
2. Why might it be easy to commit plagiarism by accident?
3. What question should you ask yourself in order to avoid plagiarism?

C Look at the following situations. Do you think they are describing plagiarism or not? If they are, do you think it was accidental or intentional?

1. Stacy copied a paragraph from a travel website and pasted it into her essay about Aruba. She put it into quotation marks and included the name and link for the website.
2. John works for a bank. He copied a paragraph from a website. He changed some words and rearranged some of the sentences. He did not indicate where it came from. He used it in a brochure for the bank.
3. Julie read an article online and later wrote her own essay about the same subject. Some of her wording was exactly the same as the online article.
4. Mitch borrowed a friend's essay to get some ideas for his own. Their teacher said that their essays were almost identical.

D PAIR WORK Sometimes famous musicians get in trouble for putting out songs that sound like someone else's. Do you think this is plagiarism? What, if anything, should be done about it?

16 Reaching your goals

▶ Discuss personal accomplishments
▶ Discuss goals

1 SNAPSHOT

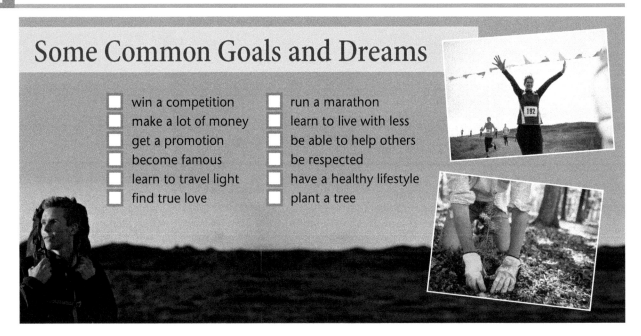

Some Common Goals and Dreams

- ☐ win a competition
- ☐ make a lot of money
- ☐ get a promotion
- ☐ become famous
- ☐ learn to travel light
- ☐ find true love

- ☐ run a marathon
- ☐ learn to live with less
- ☐ be able to help others
- ☐ be respected
- ☐ have a healthy lifestyle
- ☐ plant a tree

Which of these goals do you think are the most difficult to achieve? Which are the easiest? Why?
Do you have the same goals? Check (✓) them.
What other goals or wishes do you have?

2 PERSPECTIVES Personal accomplishments

A Listen to people talk about their accomplishments. Match the statements and the people.

1. For me, my greatest accomplishment is the feeling that I've been able to help kids develop their potential and achieve their goals. _____
2. I worked hard in school, but I never managed to get good grades. However, I've just published my first book – and it's a best seller! _____
3. Last year, I ran my first marathon. I didn't win, but I was able to finish it, and I was very proud of myself. _____
4. No one believed in me in the beginning, but I've managed to make a living from my music for the past 5 years. _____
5. I felt I had reached one of my lifetime goals when I managed to quit my nine-to-five job to make a living traveling and sharing my experiences. _____

- **a. an amateur athlete**
- **b. a teacher**
- **c. a writer**
- **d. a travel blogger**
- **e. a musician**

B GROUP WORK Do you share any similar accomplishments? Which ones?

3 GRAMMAR FOCUS

GRAMMAR PLUS see page 147

Talking about past accomplishments

With the simple past

I **managed** to quit my nine-to-five job two years ago.

I **didn't manage** to get good grades in school.

I **was able** to finish the marathon last year.

I **wasn't able** to travel much on my last job.

With the present perfect

I**'ve managed** to make a living with my music.

I **haven't managed** to record an album yet.

I**'ve been able** to help kids achieve their goals.

I **haven't been able** to achieve many of my goals.

A What are some of your latest accomplishments? Complete the statements with *have*, *haven't*, *was*, or *wasn't* to make them true for you.

1. I _____ managed to eat a healthy diet.
2. I _____ been able to help others.
3. I _____ met the person who's right for me.
4. I _____ made an important career move.
5. I _____ able to get a degree.
6. I _____ learned important life skills.

B PAIR WORK Compare your sentences in part A. What accomplishments do you have in common?

C GROUP WORK Complete the statements with your own information. Then share them with your classmates.

I have been able to _____.   I haven't been able to _____.

I have managed to _____.   I haven't managed to _____.

A: I've managed to take a trip abroad.

B: What countries did you visit?

A: I went to New Zealand three years ago.

C: Really? I've always wanted to go to New Zealand. How did you like it?

4 PRONUNCIATION Stress and rhythm

A Listen and practice. Notice how stressed words and syllables occur with a regular rhythm.

   ●   ●   ●   ●   ●

I managed to accomplish a lot while I was in college.

   ●   ●   ●   ●   ●

I haven't managed to get a promotion yet.

   ●   ●   ●   ●

I was able to share my experiences with the world.

B PAIR WORK Take turns reading the sentences in the grammar box in Exercise 3. Pay attention to stress and rhythm.

5 LISTENING A different perspective

A Listen to two people answer two interview questions. Write the obstacles
they faced and what they did about them in the chart.

	Mr. Sandberg	Ms. Rowe
Obstacle		
What he or she did		
What he or she learned		

B Listen again. What did each person learn from his or her experience?
Complete the chart.

C PAIR WORK Discuss an obstacle that you managed to overcome.
What did you learn?

6 WORD POWER Antonyms

A Complete the pairs of opposites with the words in the box.
Then compare with a partner.

| compassionate | cynical | dependent | rigid | timid | unimaginative |

1. adaptable ≠ _____
2. courageous ≠ _____
3. insensitive ≠ _____

4. resourceful ≠ _____
5. self-sufficient ≠ _____
6. upbeat ≠ _____

B GROUP WORK How many words or things can you associate with each word in part A?

A: What words or things do you associate with *resourceful*?
B: Capable.
C: Good at solving problems.

7 DISCUSSION Inspirational sayings

A Read the quotes. Which one inspires you the most?

1. The greatest pleasure in life is doing what people say you can't do.
2. Discipline is the bridge between goals and achievements.
3. No matter what you have achieved, somebody helped you.
4. Fall down seven times, stand up eight.
5. Success isn't about how much money you make. It's about the difference you make in people's lives.

B GROUP WORK Discuss and justify your choices.

A: I like the first quote because, even though my friends weren't sure I could do it,
I managed to graduate from high school early. That felt great!
B: You must have been resourceful! But someone helped you, too, didn't they?
C: That's why I like the third quote. No one achieves anything all on their own.

8 CONVERSATION Where do you see yourself?

▶ **A** Listen and practice.

Interviewer: Tell me a bit more about yourself. What's your greatest accomplishment?

Mike: I think my most important accomplishment was the development of a mobile app during my internship last summer.

Interviewer: And did you manage to finish the project?

Mike: Yes, I was able to deliver the app before the end of my internship, and it has already received lots of positive reviews from customers.

Interviewer: That's interesting. And where do you see yourself in five years?

Mike: Well, I know your company already hires remote workers, and that's one of my goals for the future. So, five years from now, I hope I'll be working from my laptop in some tropical country . . . a true digital nomad.

Interviewer: I see. And what do you hope you'll have achieved by then?

Mike: I'd like to have developed many other successful apps. And I hope I'll have seen more of the world.

B CLASS ACTIVITY What do you think of Mike's answers? How would you have answered the interviewer's questions?

9 GRAMMAR FOCUS

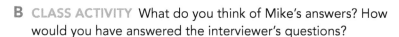

▶ **Describing goals and possible future accomplishments**

With the future perfect	With *would like to have* + past participle
What do you hope you**'ll have achieved**?	**What would you like to have** achieved?
I hope I**'ll have seen** more of the world.	I**'d like to have developed** many successful apps.

GRAMMAR PLUS *see page 147*

A What are some goals you would like to have accomplished in the future? Complete the sentences.

1. By this time next year, I hope I'll have . . .
2. Three years from now, I'd like to have . . .
3. In 10 years, I'd like to have . . .
4. By the time I'm 60, I hope I'll have . . .

B PAIR WORK Compare your sentences. What goals do you have in common?

A: By this time next year, I hope I'll have finished my English course.

B: Me, too. And I'd like to have spent some time in an English-speaking country, like . . .

Montreal, Canada

10 LISTENING My dream career

▶ **A** Listen to three young people describe their plans for the future. What do they hope they will have achieved by the time they're 30?

	1. Hugo	2. Erin	3. Danny
What they hope they'll have achieved			
Their reasons			

▶ **B** Listen again. Why does each person have his or her specific dream? List one reason for each person.

C PAIR WORK Who do you think has the most realistic expectations? the least realistic? Why?

11 INTERCHANGE 16 A digital nomad

Are you ready to work remotely? Take a quiz and find out.
Go to Interchange 16 on page 131.

12 WRITING A personal statement for an application

A Imagine you are applying to a school or for a job that requires a personal statement. Use these questions to organize your ideas. Make notes and then write a draft.

1. What has your greatest accomplishment been? Has it changed you in any way? How?
2. What are some interesting or unusual facts about yourself that make you a good choice for the job or school?
3. What is something you hope to have achieved 10 years from now? When, why, and how will you reach this goal? Will achieving it change you? Why or why not?

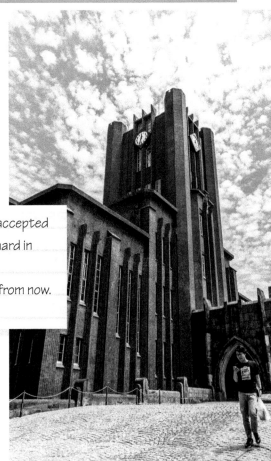

> I think my greatest accomplishment has been getting accepted at a top university in my country. I've always worked very hard in school, and I've had some truly amazing teachers who . . .
> There are two things I'd like to have achieved 10 years from now. First, I hope I'll have made a good start on my career . . .

B GROUP WORK Share your statements and discuss each person's accomplishments and goals. Who has the most unusual accomplishment or goal? the most realistic? the most ambitious?

A Scan the article. Where is Michael Edwards from? What sport did he participate in?

Soaring Like an Eagle

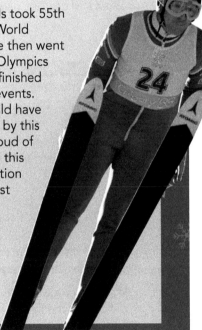

Being highly successful in any field is pretty rare. It takes a combination of natural talent, luck, determination, and plenty of outside support for someone to make it big in sports, entertainment, or business. But what if competing is all that matters to you, whether you are likely to succeed or not? This was the goal of Michael "Eddie the Eagle" Edwards, and that he reached that goal was an amazing achievement.

Born in the U.K. in 1963, Michael was an enthusiastic downhill skier whose dream was to compete for Britain in world-class competitions. He would have liked to represent his country in the 1984 Winter Olympics, but there was a large number of downhill competitors, and Edwards didn't qualify. Seeing his chance elsewhere, he switched to ski jumping. Ski jumping training didn't cost nearly as much, and there was no competition for a place on the British team.

But a number of hurdles could have meant the end of Edwards's dream. He weighed more than most competitors, which put him at a disadvantage. He had no financial support for his training. Poor eyesight meant that he had to wear glasses under his goggles – not a good thing when they steamed up at high altitudes. But he didn't let any of this discourage him. He saw himself as a true lover of the sport who simply wanted the chance to compete. Winning wasn't the point. Having the opportunity to try was all he cared about. And nothing could stop him from trying.

In the end, Edwards took 55th place in the 1987 World Championships. He then went on to the Calgary Olympics in 1988, where he finished last in both of his events. Many athletes would have been embarrassed by this result, but he is proud of his achievement to this day. His determination to persevere against all the odds made him a global hero, and in 2016, the inspiring film *Eddie the Eagle* was made about his life.

B Read the article. Answer the questions.

1. According to the writer, how often do people become highly successful?
2. What were two disadvantages that Michael Edwards overcame?
3. How did Edwards do at the Calgary Olympics in 1988?

C Choose the correct answers.

1. Michael Edwards chose ski jumping instead of downhill skiing because . . .
   a. it took less skill.
   b. the equipment was cheaper.
   c. there were few British ski jumpers.

2. After the Calgary Olympics, Edwards . . .
   a. felt he had reached his goal.
   b. was embarrassed by his results.
   c. was glad it was over.

3. Michael Edwards is outstanding because of . . .
   a. his determination to win.
   b. his ability to overcome physical disabilities.
   c. his enthusiasm for the sport.

D **PAIR WORK** Would you compete in something if you knew you were likely to lose? Why or why not?

SELF-ASSESSMENT

How well can you do these things? Check (✓) the boxes.

I can . . .	Very well	OK	A little
Give recommendations and opinions about rules (Ex. 1)	☐	☐	☐
Understand and express opinions, and seek agreement (Ex. 2)	☐	☐	☐
Describe qualities necessary to achieve particular goals (Ex. 3)	☐	☐	☐
Ask about and describe personal achievements and goals (Ex. 4)	☐	☐	☐

1 DISCUSSION It's the rule.

A **PAIR WORK** What kinds of rules do you think should be made for these places? Talk with your partner and make three rules for each. (Have fun! Don't make your rules too serious.)

office   public pool
a health club   an apartment building

B **GROUP WORK** Join another pair. Share your ideas. Do they agree?

A: Office workers should all be required to wear the same outfit.
B: That sounds interesting. Why?
A: Well, for one thing, people wouldn't need to spend so much money on clothes.

2 LISTENING My city

A Listen to people give opinions about their city. Check (✓) the correct responses to agree with their statements.

1. ☐ Yes, it should.
   ☐ No, it shouldn't.

2. ☐ Yes, it is.
   ☐ No, it isn't.

3. ☐ Yes, they are.
   ☐ No, there aren't.

4. ☐ Yes, it does.
   ☐ Yes, they do.

5. ☐ Yes, we do.
   ☐ No, we don't.

6. ☐ No, there isn't.
   ☐ Yes, it is.

B **PAIR WORK** Come up with three more opinions about your city with a partner. Ask your classmates and see if they agree or disagree.

A: There aren't enough nightlife options for teenagers, are there?
B: No, there aren't!

3 DISCUSSION Do you have what it takes?

A **GROUP WORK** What qualities are needed if you want to accomplish these goals? Decide on two qualities for each goal.

Goals	Qualities		
start your own business	adaptable	dependent	self-sufficient
live abroad for a year	compassionate	insensitive	timid
make a low-budget movie	courageous	resourceful	unimaginative
hike across your country	cynical	rigid	upbeat

A: To start your own business, you need to be resourceful.

B: Yeah, and you should be courageous too.

B **PAIR WORK** Does your partner have what it takes to accomplish the goals in part A? Interview him or her and find out.

A: Do you think you're resourceful?

B: Yes, I think so. I'm usually good at solving problems.

4 ROLE PLAY Students' profiles

Student A: Student B is going to interview you for the school website.
Think about your accomplishments and goals.
Then answer the questions.

Student B: You are interviewing Student A for the school website.
Add two questions to the notebook paper below.
Then start the interview.

Change roles and try the role play again.

> What have you managed to accomplish in school?
> What would you like to have achieved by the time you graduate?
>
> Are you happy with your home?
> Do you hope you will move someday?
> Where would you like to live?
>
> Have you been able to accomplish a lot in your career?
> Where do you hope you'll be in 5 years?

WHAT'S NEXT?

Look at your Self-assessment again. Do you need to review anything?

This page is intentionally left blank

Interchange activities

A PAIR WORK Read these comments made by parents. Why do you think they feel this way? Think of two arguments to support each point of view.

Our son wants to go camping with his friends alone. No way!

Our son wants to stay out until midnight. We think that's way too late.

Our son wants to have his hair cut at an expensive salon. What's wrong with a regular barber?

Our son wants a new laptop, but we just bought him one last year. He can have it upgraded instead.

If our daughter insists on having her nails done at a nail salon, she has to pay for it herself.

Our daughter wants to sleep over at friends' houses on weeknights. Absolutely not!

Our daughter wants to have her ears pierced. We're totally against that.

Regardless of the color, we refuse to let our daughter get her hair dyed.

A: Why do you think they won't let their son go camping with his friends?
B: They probably think he's too young to take care of himself.
A: They may also feel that he . . .

B PAIR WORK Discuss the parents' decisions. Think of arguments for and against their points of view.

A: I think the parents should let their son go camping with his friends.
B: Why?
A: Because his friends are going, and he needs to learn to take care of himself.
B: I don't agree. I think he's too young. Teens shouldn't travel without an adult.

C CLASS ACTIVITY Take a vote. Do you agree with the parents? Why?

Student A

A **PAIR WORK** Ask your partner these questions. Put a check (✓) if your partner gives the correct answer. (The correct answers are in **bold**.)

Frida Kahlo

Volkswagen Beetle

Alexander Fleming

TEST YOUR KNOWLEDGE

☐ 1. What nationality was the painter Frida Kahlo? Was she Spanish, **Mexican**, or Argentinian?

☐ 2. What was the first capital of the United States? Was it **Philadelphia**, New York, or Boston?

☐ 3. Who played 007 in the first James Bond movie? Was it Roger Moore, **Sean Connery**, or Pierce Brosnan?

☐ 4. When was the first Volkswagen Beetle car built? Was it during the 1920s, **1930s**, or 1940s?

☐ 5. Was Nelson Mandela a political activist from India, Angola, or **South Africa**?

☐ 6. When did the British return Hong Kong to China? Was it in 1987, **1997**, or 2007?

☐ 7. Who discovered penicillin? Was it **Alexander Fleming**, Charles Darwin, or Albert Einstein?

☐ 8. Which planet is closest to the sun? Is it Mars, **Mercury**, or Venus?

☐ 9. What Italian astronomer invented the thermometer in 1593? Was it Copernicus, Isaac Newton, or **Galileo**?

☐ 10. When did the first MP3 player hit the market in the US? Was it in 1978, 1988, or **1998**?

B **PAIR WORK** Answer the questions your partner asks you. Then compare quizzes. Who has the most correct answers?

C **CLASS ACTIVITY** Think of three more questions of your own. Can the rest of the class answer them?

A PAIR WORK Play the board game. Follow these instructions.

1. Use small pieces of paper with your initials on them as markers.

2. Take turns tossing a coin:

 Move one space.

Heads

 Move two spaces.

Tails

3. When you land on a space, tell your partner what is true. Then say how things would have been different. For example:

   "When I was younger, I didn't pay attention in class. If I had paid attention in class, I would have gotten better grades."

   OR

   "When I was younger, I paid attention in class. If I hadn't paid attention in class, I wouldn't have won a scholarship."

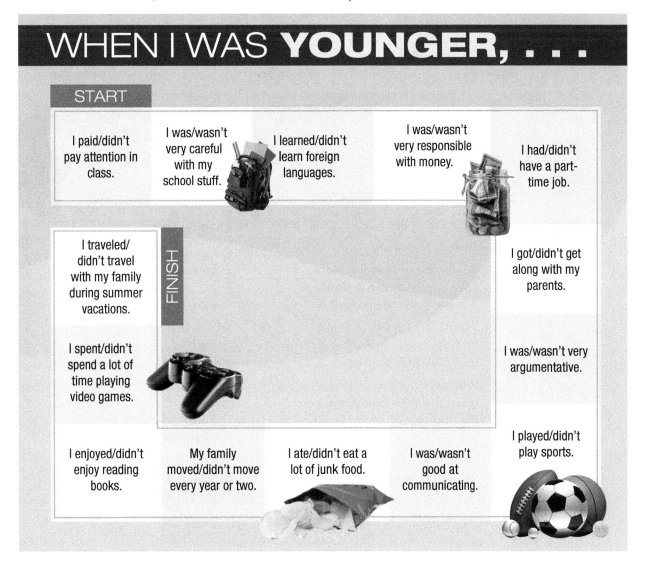

WHEN I WAS **YOUNGER, . . .**

START

I paid/didn't pay attention in class.

I was/wasn't very careful with my school stuff.

I learned/didn't learn foreign languages.

I was/wasn't very responsible with money.

I had/didn't have a part-time job.

FINISH

I traveled/didn't travel with my family during summer vacations.

I got/didn't get along with my parents.

I spent/didn't spend a lot of time playing video games.

I was/wasn't very argumentative.

I enjoyed/didn't enjoy reading books.

My family moved/didn't move every year or two.

I ate/didn't eat a lot of junk food.

I was/wasn't good at communicating.

I played/didn't play sports.

B CLASS ACTIVITY Who was responsible when they were younger? Who was rebellious? Tell the class.

Student B

A PAIR WORK Answer the questions your partner asks you.

B PAIR WORK Ask your partner these questions. Put a check (✓) if your partner gives the correct answer. (The correct answers are in **bold**.) Then compare quizzes. Who has the most correct answers?

Mona Lisa

a compass

Berlin Wall

TEST YOUR KNOWLEDGE

☐ 1. What was the former name of New York City? Was it New England, New London, or **New Amsterdam**?

☐ 2. What artist painted the *Mona Lisa*? Was it **Leonardo da Vinci**, Michelangelo, or Raphael?

☐ 3. When did Walt Disney make his first cartoon movie? Was it in 1920, **1937**, or 1947?

☐ 4. Who used the first magnetic compass? Was it **the Chinese**, the Portuguese, or the Dutch?

☐ 5. Constantinople was an earlier name of what city? Was it Cairo, Mumbai, or **Istanbul**?

☐ 6. When did the Berlin Wall come down? Was it in 1979, **1989**, or 1999?

☐ 7. Where was Marie Curie, the first woman to receive a Nobel Prize, born? Was it in **Poland**, France, or England?

☐ 8. Who was the first human in space? Was it **Yuri Gagarin**, Neil Armstrong, or John Glenn?

☐ 9. What did Thomas Edison invent in 1879? Was it the television, the telephone, or the **lightbulb**?

☐ 10. In which year did Mexico gain its independence? Was it in 1721, **1821**, or 1921?

C CLASS ACTIVITY Think of three more questions of your own. Can the rest of the class answer them?

A PAIR WORK Read these popular slogans for products.
Match the slogans with the product types.

1. Think different. _____
2. Unforgettable happens here. _____
3. Taste the feeling. _____
4. All the news that's fit to print. _____
5. Impossible is nothing. _____
6. Bet you can't eat just one. _____
7. Stay with us, and feel like home. _____
8. Reach out and touch someone. _____
9. I'm loving it. _____
10. Live in your world. Play in ours. _____
11. Melts in your mouth, not in your hands. _____
12. Built for the road ahead. _____

a. a soft drink
b. a technology company
c. an amusement park
d. sports clothing
e. potato chips
f. a daily newspaper
g. fast food
h. automobiles
i. a game console
j. a hotel
k. a telephone service
l. chocolate candy

B PAIR WORK Join another pair and compare your answers.
Then check your answers at the bottom of the page.

C GROUP WORK Think of a product. Then create your own slogan for it and
add a logo. Consider a design and colors that are suitable for the product.

A: Any ideas for a product?
B: What about an online store for used toys?
C: Sounds interesting. Let's try to think of some catchy slogans.
D: How about, "Play again!"? Or maybe . . .

D CLASS ACTIVITY Present your slogans to the class.
Who has the catchiest ones?

1. b; 2. c; 3. a; 4. f; 5. d; 6. e; 7. j; 8. k; 9. g; 10. i; 11. l; 12. h

A PAIR WORK What do you think might have happened in each situation? Talk about possibilities for each situation.

Pete made a fortune in the stock market. He's now working at a burger joint.

Lisa went grocery shopping yesterday afternoon. She hasn't come back home yet.

Jim was the best salesperson in the company for the past 10 years. He just got fired.

Clara had everything ready for her dream vacation in Tahiti. She's on the bus heading to her parents' home.

A: Maybe Pete made some bad investments.

B: Or he might have spent all his money on . . .

useful expressions	
Maybe he/she was . . . when . . .	He/She may have . . . when . . .
Or perhaps he/she was . . .	He/She might have . . .

B GROUP WORK Agree on one explanation for each situation and share it with the class. Be ready to answer any questions.

A Prepare to play a guessing game.

- Write the names of five celebrities on slips of paper. Names can include people in history, movie stars, singers, politicians, writers, etc.
- Mix all the slips in a bag.

Adele

B GROUP WORK Each player takes turns picking a slip for his or her group to guess.

A: She's a celebrity who was born in London.
B: Is she a movie star?
A: No, she's a singer and songwriter who has a beautiful voice.
C: I think I know the answer. It's . . .

C CLASS ACTIVITY Which celebrities were easier to guess? Which were the most difficult? Who gave the best clues?

Nico Rosberg

Sofia Vergara

Albert Einstein

Sally Ride

A **PAIR WORK** What punishment (if any) is appropriate for each possible offense? Why? Complete the chart.

OFFENSE	PUNISHMENT
1 parking in a disabled parking space without a permit	
2 posting offensive comments online	
3 leaving trash on public streets	
4 riding the subway without paying the fare	
5 failing to clean up after a dog	
6 pickpocketing	
7 scratching paint off another person's car	
8 crossing the street in dangerous places	
9 driving without a seat belt	
10 riding a motorcycle without a helmet	
11 hacking into a government computer	
12 _____ (your own idea)	

A: What do you think should be done about people who park in a disabled parking space without a permit?
B: They should be required to pay a heavy fine because it may cause problems for people with disabilities.
A: I don't agree. I think . . .

B **GROUP WORK** Join another pair of students. Then compare and discuss your lists. Do you agree or disagree? Try to convince each other that you are right!

possible punishments

receive a warning
spend some time in jail
pay a fine
lose a driver's license
get suspended
do community service
be banned from using the Internet

A PAIR WORK Interview your partner. Would he or she be a happy digital nomad?

Is the digital nomad lifestyle **right for you?**

Do you dream of working from a beach paradise? Are you ready to hit the road and make a living while traveling the world? Take our quiz and find out.

1. Have you traveled much before?
   - ☐ **a.** I've traveled with my family in our country.
   - ☐ **b.** Not yet, but I hope to have seen more of the world by the time I retire.
   - ☐ **c.** I've been to a couple of continents and seen some amazing things!

2. Are you resourceful?
   - ☐ **a.** Well, I can always count on my friends to help me when I need it.
   - ☐ **b.** Yes, and I can always find the answers I need on the Internet.
   - ☐ **c.** Yes, I'm good at finding opportunities everywhere.

3. When you pack for a long weekend, what do you take with you?
   - ☐ **a.** A big suitcase with everything I might need – you never know what might happen.
   - ☐ **b.** A small bag with the essentials.
   - ☐ **c.** A toothbrush and a change of clothes. I like to travel light.

4. Are you flexible and adaptable?
   - ☐ **a.** I try to be, but I don't always succeed.
   - ☐ **b.** Yes, if you give me some time to adjust.
   - ☐ **c.** Definitely. I've managed to survive under the most challenging circumstances.

5. Have you ever traveled all by yourself?
   - ☐ **a.** Of course not. I need family and friends around at all times.
   - ☐ **b.** No, but I think I'd enjoy it.
   - ☐ **c.** Sure. I often take vacations alone. It's a great opportunity to meet new people.

6. Are you ready to give up a fixed salary?
   - ☐ **a.** No. I need to have a steady income. It's important for me to know how much money I'll be making for the next 12 months.
   - ☐ **b.** Well, I can live on very little money – I've done it before.
   - ☐ **c.** I'm good at managing my money, and I always have some savings, so that wouldn't be a problem.

7. Are you self-motivated, or do you depend on others to get you going?
   - ☐ **a.** I need to know that my boss or my teachers are around and that I can count on them.
   - ☐ **b.** It depends. If I'm really involved with a project, I'm more independent; if not . . .
   - ☐ **c.** Definitely. I know what I have to do, and I always finish the work on time.

8. How do you feel about changes?
   - ☐ **a.** I like to have a set routine. Changes make me feel uncomfortable.
   - ☐ **b.** They can be a challenge, but they also help me grow.
   - ☐ **c.** Changes are always welcome. New things inspire and motivate me.

Score the quiz by counting the number of a's, b's, and c's.

Mostly a's: The digital nomad lifestyle is not for you.

Mostly b's: You'd probably be happy being a digital nomad, but you might miss your current life.

Mostly c's: What are you doing here? Go grab your things and hit the road!

B CLASS ACTIVITY Compare your findings. Who is ready to become a digital nomad?

Grammar plus

1 Get or have something done   page 59

> ■ Sentences with *get/have* + object + past participle are passive. BUT Don't use any form of *be* before the past participle: Where can I **have** my watch **fixed**? (NOT: Where can I have my watch ~~be~~ fixed?)

Rewrite the statements as questions with *Where can I get/have . . . ?*
Then complete B's answers with the information in parentheses.

1. I want to have someone shorten these pants.
   A: _Where can I have these pants shortened?_
   B: _You can have them shortened at Tim's Tailoring._ (at Tim's Tailoring)
2. I need to get someone to repair my computer.
   A: _____
   B: _____ (at Hackers Inc.)
3. I need to have someone prepare my taxes.
   A: _____
   B: _____ (by my accountant)
4. I'd like to get someone to cut my hair.
   A: _____
   B: _____ (at Beauty Barn)
5. I need to have someone paint my apartment.
   A: _____
   B: _____ (by Peter the Painter)

2 Making suggestions   page 61

> ■ Use the base form of a verb – without *to* – after *Maybe you could . . .* and *Why don't you . . . ?*: Maybe you could **join** a book club. (NOT: Maybe you could ~~to~~ join a book club.) Why don't you **join** a book club? (NOT: Why don't you ~~to~~ join a book club?)

Complete the conversations with the correct form of the verbs in parentheses.

A: I'm having trouble meeting people here in the city. Any ideas?

B: I know it's hard. Why don't you _____ (join) a gym? That's usually a good place to meet people. Or maybe you could _____ (take) a class at the community college.

A: What about _____ (check out) the personal ads? Do you think that's a good way to meet people?

B: I wouldn't recommend doing that. People never tell the truth in those ads. But it might be a good idea _____ (find) a sports team. Have you thought about _____ (play) a team sport – maybe baseball or volleyball?

A: I'm not very good at most sports, but I used to play tennis.

B: There you go! One option is _____ (look up) tennis clubs in the city and see which clubs have teams people can join.

A: Now, that's a great idea. And I could always use the exercise!

UNIT 10

1 Referring to time in the past page 65

- Use *since* with a particular time: The UN has been in existence **since** 1945.
  Use *for* with a duration of time: The UN has been in existence **for** about the last 70 years.
- Use *in* and *during* with a specific period of time: Rock 'n' roll became popular **in/during** the 1950s.
- Use *from* and *to* to describe when something began and ended: World War II lasted **from** 1939 **to** 1945.

Complete the conversation with the words in the box. (Use some of the words more than once.)

ago	during	for	from	in	since	to

A: Hey, Dad. Did you use to listen to the Beatles?

B: Of course. In fact, I just listened to one of their records a few days _____*ago*_____.
Do you realize that the Beatles's music has influenced other musicians _____
over 50 years? They were the greatest!

A: Well, I just found some interesting information about them. I'll read it to you: "The
Beatles were a well-known British band _____ the 1960s. They performed
together _____ 10 years – _____ 1960 _____
1970. _____ 2003, the Beatles released *Let it Be*, even though one of
the original members had been dead _____ 1980 and another had died
_____ 2001. The original album had been recorded _____ 1969
and was in the studio safe _____ 34 years before the new, remixed album
was released."

B: That *is* interesting. It's pretty amazing that people have listened to the Beatles
_____ both the twentieth and the twenty-first centuries, isn't it?

2 Predicting the future with *will* page 67

- In sentences referring to time, the preposition *by* means "not later than." Don't
  confuse *by* with *within*, which means "some time during." Use *by* with points in
  time; use *within* with periods of time: **By** 2050, we will have eliminated starvation
  around the world. (NOT: ~~Within~~ 2050, . . .) **Within** the next five years, people will
  have invented mobile phone apps for nearly everything! (NOT: ~~By~~ the next
  five years, . . .)

Circle the correct verb forms to complete the conversation.

A: What do you think you **will do / will be doing** five years from now?

B: I'm not sure. Maybe I **will get / will have gotten** married by then. How about you?

A: I **will be finishing / will have finished** medical school, so I **will be doing / will have done**
my internship five years from now.

B: So you **won't be living / won't have lived** around here in five years, I guess. Where
do you think you **will live / will have lived**?

A: Wherever I get my internship.

1 Time clauses page 73

> ■ Use the past perfect in the main clause with *until* and *by the time*. This shows
> that one of the past events happened before the other: Until I got my driver's
> license, I **had** always **taken** public transportation. By the time I got my driver's
> license, all of my friends **had** already **gotten** theirs.

Circle the correct time expression to complete each sentence.

1. After / (**Until**) I traveled overseas, I hadn't known much about different cultures.

2. After / Before I got a full-time job, I had to live on a very limited budget.

3. By the time / Once I finished high school, I had already taken three college courses.

4. As soon as / Before I left for college, my mother turned my room into her office.

5. Once / Until I left home, I realized how much my family meant to me.

6. By the time / The moment you have a child, you feel totally responsible for him or her.

2 Expressing regret and describing hypothetical situations page 75

> ■ Conditional sentences describing hypothetical situations often refer to both the
> present and the past:
> If I**'d finished** college, I**'d have** a better job now.
>   past   present
> (NOT: If I'd finished college, I'd ~~have had~~ a better job now.)

A Write sentences with *should (not) have* to express regret about each person's situation.

1. Sarah was very argumentative with her teacher, so she had to stay after school.
   Sarah shouldn't have been argumentative with her teacher.

2. Ivan didn't save up for a car, so he still has to take public transportation.

3. Jon was very inactive when he was in college, so he gained a lot of weight.

4. Lisa didn't stay in touch with her high school classmates, so now she has very few friends.

5. Tony didn't study Spanish in school, so he's not bilingual now.

B Rewrite your sentences in part A, changing them to hypothetical situations.

1. *If Sarah hadn't been argumentative with her teacher, she wouldn't have*
   had to stay after school.

2. _____

3. _____

4. _____

5. _____

UNIT 12

1 Describing purpose page 79

> ■ Don't use *for* immediately before an infinitive: **To have** a successful business, you need a lot of luck. (NOT: ~~For~~ to have a successful business, you need a lot of luck.)

A Complete the sentences with *in order to* or *in order for*.

1. _____In order for_____ a supermarket to succeed, it has to be clean and well organized.
2. _____ stay popular, a website needs to be accurate and visually attractive.
3. _____ run a profitable furniture store, it's important to advertise on TV.
4. _____ a restaurant to stay in business, it needs to have "regulars" – customers that come often.
5. _____ establish a successful nail salon, it has to have a convenient location.
6. _____ an online business to survive, it needs to have excellent pictures of the merchandise it's selling.

B Rewrite the sentences in part A without *In order*.

1. _For a supermarket to succeed, it has to be clean and well organized._
2. _____
3. _____
4. _____
5. _____
6. _____

2 Giving reasons page 81

> ■ *Because* and *since* have the same meaning, and they can begin or end a sentence: **Because/Since** the food is always fantastic, Giorgio's is my favorite restaurant. = Giorgio's is my favorite restaurant **because/since** the food is always fantastic.
>
> ■ Don't confuse *because* and *because of*. *Because* introduces an adverb clause and is followed by a subject and verb, while *because of* is a preposition and is followed by a noun object: **Because** Giorgio's is so popular, we should get there early. Giorgio's is popular **because of** its food and service.

Circle the correct words to complete the conversation.

A: I had to go downtown today **because / because of / due to** I needed to mail a package at the post office. **Due to / For / Since** I was only a few blocks from Main Street, I went over to Martin's. Did you know that Martin's has gone out of business? I'm so upset!

B: That's too bad, but I'm not surprised. A lot of family-owned shops are closing **because / because of / since** the construction of shopping malls.

A: Yeah, and don't forget about all the megastores that are popping up everywhere. **Because / For / The reason why** people prefer to shop there is to save money. Everyone loves a megastore **because / due to / since** the low prices and the huge selection.

B: Not me! I loved Martin's **for / since / the reason that** their beautiful clothes and friendly salespeople. When you were there, you almost felt like family. You'll never get that at a megastore!

1 Past modals for degrees of certainty　page 87

> ■ Use the past modal *could have* to express possibility. BUT Use *couldn't have* when you are almost 100% sure something is impossible: I suppose he **could have gotten** stuck in traffic, but he **couldn't have forgotten** his own birthday party.

Complete the conversations with past modals *must (not) have, could (not) have,* or *may/might (not) have*. Use the degrees of certainty and the verbs in parentheses. (More than one answer may be possible.)

1. A: Yoko still hasn't called me back.

　B: She _ might not have gotten _ your message. (it's possible – not get)

2. A: What's wrong with Steven?

　B: Oh, you _____ the news. His dog ran away. (it's almost certain – not hear)

3. A: I went to see the Larsens today, but they didn't answer the door.

　B: Was their car there? If so, they _____ in the backyard. (it's possible – be)

4. A: Fabio said he was going to the party last night, but I didn't see him.

　B: Neither did I. He _____ there then. (it's not possible – not be)

5. A: I can't find my glasses, but I know I had them at work today.

　B: You _____ them at the office. (it's possible – leave)

6. A: Marc's new car looks really expensive.

　B: Yes, it does. It _____ a fortune! (it's almost certain – cost)

2 Past modals for judgments and suggestions　page 89

> ■ In advice with *would have*, the speaker means, "If I were you, . . ."

Read each situation and choose the corresponding judgment or suggestion for an alternative past action.

Situation

1. Sue forgot her boyfriend's birthday. _ b _

2. Tim got a speeding ticket. _____

3. Ruth still hasn't paid me back. _____

4. Bill lied to us. _____

5. I spent an hour making Joe dinner, and he didn't even thank me. _____

6. Carol came over for dinner empty-handed. _____

Judgment/Suggestion

a. I wouldn't have lent her money.

b. She should have put it on her calendar.

c. He should have told the truth.

d. He shouldn't have gone over the limit.

e. She should have brought something.

f. I wouldn't have cooked for him.

1 The passive to describe process page 93

> ■ The modals *have to* and *need to* must agree with the subject; other modals,
> like *may be*, have only one form: Each character **has to/needs to** be drawn by
> the animators.

Put the words in the correct order to make sentences.

1. overnight / business / A / started / small / isn't / .
   A small business isn't started overnight.

2. to / plan / business / a / written / First, / be / has / .
   _____

3. research / Next, / done / be / market / should / .
   _____

4. needs / competition / to / the / Then / identified / be / .
   _____

5. online / ads / posted / be / Classified / may / .
   _____

6. work / are / employees / hired / can / start / the / so / Finally, / .
   _____

2 Defining and non-defining relative clauses page 96

> ■ Use either *who* or *that* in defining relative clauses about people: A set designer
> is an artist **who/that** makes important contributions to a theater production. BUT
> Use only *who* in non-defining relative clauses about people: A set designer, **who**
> makes important contributions to a theater production, has to be very creative.
> (NOT: A set designer, ~~that~~ makes . . .)
>
> ■ Use commas before and after a non-defining clause: A gossip columnist**,** who
> writes about celebrities and scandals**,** often gets to go to fabulous parties.

Combine these sentences with *who* or *that*. Add a comma wherever one is necessary.

1. A cartoon animator creates animated scenes for movies and games. He or she needs
   to have a high level of technical know-how.
   A cartoon animator, who needs to have a high level of technical know-how, creates
   animated scenes for movies and games.

2. A screenwriter is a talented person. He or she develops a story idea into a movie script.
   A screenwriter is a talented person that develops a story idea into a movie script.

3. Voice-over actors are usually freelancers. They give voice to characters in animated
   movies and video games.
   _____

4. Casting directors choose an actor for each part in a movie. They have usually been
   in the movie business for a long time.
   _____

5. High-budget movies always use big stars. The stars are known around the world.
   _____

6. Movie directors are greatly respected. They "make or break" a film.
   _____

1 Giving recommendations and opinions `page 101`

> ■ *Ought to* has the same meaning as *should*, but it's more formal:
> Traffic signs **ought to** be obeyed. = Traffic signs **should** be obeyed.

A student committee is discussing rules for their school. Complete speaker B's sentences with appropriate passive modals. (More than one answer is possible.)

1. A: Students must be required to clean off the cafeteria tables after lunch.
   B: I disagree. Students ___*shouldn't be required*___ to do that. That's what the cafeteria workers are paid to do.

2. A: Teachers shouldn't be allowed to park in the student parking lot.
   B: Why not? Teachers _____ to park wherever a space is available. After all, they're here for us.

3. A: A rule has to be made to ban the use of cell phones in school.
   B: I don't think a rule _____. Students may need their phones for emergency purposes.

4. A: Students mustn't be permitted to use calculators during math exams.
   B: Sometimes we _____ to use them, especially when we're being tested on more complicated concepts than simple arithmetic.

5. A: Something has got to be done to control the noise in the hallways.
   B: Students _____ to talk to each other between classes, though. They aren't disturbing anyone when classes aren't in session.

6. A: Teachers must be required to remind students about important exams.
   B: That's unnecessary. On the contrary, students _____ to follow the syllabus and check important dates on the course websites.

2 Tag questions for opinions `page 103`

> ■ Tag questions added to statements in the simple present and simple past use the corresponding auxiliary verb in the tag: You **agree** with me, **don't** you? You **don't agree** with me, **do** you? You **paid** the rent, **didn't** you? You **didn't pay** the electric bill, **did** you?

Check (✓) the sentences if the tag questions are correct. If they're incorrect, write the correct tag questions.

1. Food is getting more and more expensive, ~~is it~~? _____*isn't it*_____
2. Supermarkets should try to keep their prices down, shouldn't they? _____✓_____
3. People don't buy as many fresh fruits and vegetables as they used to, don't they? _____
4. We have to buy healthy food for our children, don't we? _____
5. Many children go to school hungry, won't they? _____
6. Some people can't afford to eat meat every day, don't they? _____
7. We can easily live without eating meat every day, can we? _____
8. A lot of people are having a hard time making ends meet these days, haven't they? _____

1 Talking about past accomplishments page 107

> ■ When talking about past accomplishments and including a specific time, use the simple past – not the present perfect: I **was** able to complete my degree last year. (NOT: I've been able to complete my degree last year.)

Complete the sentences about people's accomplishments. Use the verbs in parentheses. (More than one answer is possible.)

In the last 5 years, Ana . . .

1. <u>managed to finish</u>   (finish) college.
2. _____   (pay) all her college loans.
3. _____   (start) her own company.
4. _____   (move) to the city.
5. _____   (make) some new friends.

In the past year, Bill . . .

6. _____   (buy) a new car.
7. _____   (take) a vacation.
8. _____   (get) a promotion at work.
9. _____   (learn) to cook.
10. _____   (visit) his grandparents in the south.

2 Describing goals and possible future accomplishments page 109

> ■ When talking about future accomplishments and goals, use *in* to refer to a period of time: I hope I'll find a new job **in** the next two months. Use *by* to talk about a time limit in the future: I hope I'll find a new job **by** the end of September. = I hope I'll find a new job not later than the end of September.

Complete the conversation. Use the verbs in parentheses. (Sometimes more than one answer is possible.)

Louise: So, Mike, what do you hope you <u>will have accomplished</u> (accomplish) five years from now?

Mike: I hope I _____ (complete) medical school, and I _____ (start) my residence in a good hospital.

Louise: What about your personal goals? What _____ (achieve) by then?

Mike: Well, I _____ (meet) that special someone, and, maybe, I _____ (get) married by then. What about you? What are your goals?

Louise: Well, I hope I _____ (finish) culinary school in the next five years, and I _____ (manage) to work with some famous chef.

Mike: Good plan! What about opening your own restaurant?

Louise: That will take some more time, but by the time I'm 35, I hope I _____ (open) my own bistro – Chez Louise.

Mike: I can hardly wait. I just love your food.

Unit 16 Grammar plus **147**

Grammar plus answer key

Unit 9

1 Get or have something done
2. A: Where can I get/have my computer repaired?
   B: You can get/have it repaired at Hackers Inc.
3. A: Where can I get/have my taxes prepared?
   B: You can get/have them prepared by my accountant.
4. A: Where can I get/have my hair cut?
   B: You can get/have it cut at Beauty Barn.
5. A: Where can I get/have my apartment painted?
   B: You can get/have it painted by Peter the Painter.

2 Making suggestions
A: I'm having trouble meeting people here in the city. Any ideas?
B: I know it's hard. Why don't you **join** a gym? That's usually a good place to meet people. Or maybe you could **take** a class at the community college.
A: What about **checking out** the personal ads? Do you think that's a good way to meet people?
B: I wouldn't recommend doing that. People never tell the truth in those ads. But it might be a good idea **to find** a sports team. Have you thought about **playing** a team sport – maybe baseball or volleyball?
A: I'm not very good at most sports, but I used to play tennis.
B: There you go! One option is **to look up** tennis clubs in the city and see which clubs have teams people can join.
A: Now, that's a great idea. And I could always use the exercise!

Unit 10

1 Referring to time in the past
A: Hey, Dad. Did you use to listen to the Beatles?
B: Of course. In fact, I just listened to one of their records a few days **ago**. Do you realize that the Beatles's music has influenced other musicians **for** over 50 years? They were the greatest!
A: Well, I just found some interesting information about them. I'll read it to you: "The Beatles were a well-known British band **during/in** the 1960s. They performed together **for** 10 years – **from** 1960 **to** 1970. **In** 2003, the Beatles released a new version of their classic album *Let it Be*, even though one of the original members had been dead **since** 1980 and another had died **in** 2001. The original album had been recorded **in** 1969 and was in the studio safe **for** 34 years before the new, remixed album was released."
B: That *is* interesting. It's pretty amazing that people have listened to the Beatles **in** both the twentieth and the twenty-first centuries, isn't it?

2 Predicting the future with *will*
A: What do you think you **will be doing** five years from now?
B: I'm not sure. Maybe I **will have gotten** married by then. How about you?
A: I **will have finished** medical school, so I **will be doing** my internship five years from now.
B: So you **won't be living** around here in five years, I guess. Where do you think you **will live**?
A: Wherever I get my internship.

Unit 11

1 Time clauses
2. **Before** I got a full-time job, I had to live on a very limited budget.
3. **By the time** I finished high school, I had already taken three college courses.
4. **As soon as** I left for college, my mother turned my room into her office.
5. **Once** I left home, I realized how much my family meant to me.
6. **The moment** you have a child, you feel totally responsible for him or her.

2 Expressing regret and describing hypothetical situations
A
2. Ivan should have saved up for a car.
3. Jon shouldn't have been inactive when he was in college.
4. Lisa should have stayed in touch with her high school classmates.
5. Tony should have studied Spanish in school.
B
Answers may vary. Some possible answers:
2. If Ivan had saved up for a car, he wouldn't have to take public transportation.
3. If Jon hadn't been inactive when he was in college, he wouldn't have gained a lot of weight.
4. If Lisa had stayed in touch with her high school classmates, she wouldn't have very few friends.
5. If Tony had studied Spanish in school, he would be bilingual now.

Unit 12

1 Describing purpose
A
2. **In order to** stay popular, a website needs to be accurate and visually attractive.
3. **In order to** run a profitable furniture store, it's important to advertise on TV.
4. **In order for** a restaurant to stay in business, it needs to have "regulars" – customers that come often.
5. **In order to** establish a successful nail salon, it has to have a convenient location.
6. **In order for** an online business to survive, it needs to have excellent pictures of the merchandise it's selling.
B
2. To stay popular, a website needs to be accurate and visually attractive.
3. To run a profitable furniture store, it's important to advertise on TV.
4. For a restaurant to stay in business, it needs to have "regulars" – customers that come often.
5. To establish a successful nail salon, it has to have a convenient location.
6. For an online business to survive, it needs to have excellent pictures of the merchandise it's selling.

2 Giving reasons
A: I had to go downtown today **because** I needed to mail a package at the post office. **Since** I was only a few blocks from Main Street, I went over to Martin's. Did you know that Martin's has gone out of business? I'm so upset!
B: That's too bad, but I'm not surprised. A lot of family-owned shops are closing **because of** the construction of shopping malls.
A: Yeah, and don't forget about all the megastores that are popping up everywhere. **The reason why** people prefer to shop there is to save money. Everyone loves a megastore **due to** the low prices and the huge selection.
B: Not me! I loved Martin's **for** their beautiful clothes and friendly salespeople. When you were there, you almost felt like family. You'll never get that at a megastore!

Unit 13

1 Past modals for degrees of certainty
Answers may vary. Some possible answers:
2. A: What's wrong with Steven?
   B: Oh, you **must not have heard** the news. His dog ran away.
3. A: I went to see the Larsens today, but they didn't answer the door.
   B: Was their car there? If so, they **could have been** in the backyard.
4. A: Fabio said he was going to the party last night, but I didn't see him.
   B: Neither did I. He **couldn't have been** there then.
5. A: I can't find my glasses, but I know I had them at work today.
   B: You **might have left** them at the office.
6. A: Marc's new car looks really expensive.
   B: Yes, it does. It **must have cost** a fortune!

2 Past modals for judgments and suggestions
2. d   3. a   4. c   5. f   6. e

Unit 14

1 The passive to describe process
2. First, a business plan has to be written.
3. Next, market research should be done.
4. Then the competition needs to be identified.
5. Classified ads may be posted online.
6. Finally, employees are hired so the work can start.

2 Defining and non-defining relative clauses
3. Voice-over actors, who give voice to characters in animated movies and video games, are usually freelancers.
4. Casting directors, who have usually been in the movie business for a long time, choose an actor for each part in a movie.
5. High-budget movies always use big stars that are known around the world.
6. Movie directors, who "make or break" a film, are greatly respected.

Unit 15

1 Giving recommendations and opinions
Answers may vary. Some possible answers:
2. A: Teachers shouldn't be allowed to park in the student parking lot.
   B: Why not? Teachers **should be allowed** to park wherever a space is available. After all, they're here for us.
3. A: A rule has to be made to ban the use of cell phones in school.
   B: I don't think a rule **has to be made**. Students may need their phones for emergency purposes.
4. A: Students mustn't be permitted to use calculators during math exams.
   B: Sometimes we **should be permitted** to use them, especially when we're being tested on more complicated concepts than simple arithmetic.
5. A: Something has got to be done to control the noise in the hallways.
   B: Students **should be allowed** to talk to each other between classes, though. They aren't disturbing anyone when classes aren't in session.
6. A: Teachers must be required to remind students about important exams.
   B: That's unnecessary. On the contrary, students **should be required** to follow the syllabus and check important dates on the course websites.

2 Tag questions for opinions
3. do they   6. can they
4. ✓   7. can't we
5. don't they   8. aren't they

Unit 16

1 Talking about past accomplishments
Answers may vary. Some possible answers:
2. has managed to pay
3. has been able to start
4. was able to move
5. managed to make
6. was able to buy
7. has managed to take
8. has managed to get
9. has been able to learn
10. has managed to visit

2 Describing goals and possible future accomplishments
Louise: So, Mike, what do you hope you will have accomplished five years from now?
Mike: I hope I'**ll have completed** medical school and I'**ll have started / 'd like to have started** my residence in a good hospital.
Louise: What about your personal goals? What **would you like to have achieved** by then?
Mike: Well, I'**d like to have met** that special someone, and, maybe I'**ll have gotten** married by then. What about you? What are your goals?
Louise: Well, I hope I'**ll have finished** culinary school in five years, and I'**ll have managed / 'd like to have managed** to work with some famous chef.
Mike: Good plan! What about opening your own restaurant?
Louise: That will take some more time, but by the time I'm 35, I hope I'**ll have opened** my own bistro – Chez Louise.
Mike: I can hardly wait. I just love your food.

Credits

The authors and publishers acknowledge the following sources of copyright material and are grateful for the permissions granted. While every effort has been made, it has not always been possible to identify the sources of all the material used, or to trace all copyright holders. If any omissions are brought to our notice, we will be happy to include the appropriate acknowledgements on reprinting and in the next update to the digital edition, as applicable.

Key: Ex = Exercise, T = Top, B = Below, C = Centre, CR = Centre Right, TR = Top Right, BR = Below Right, TL = Top Left, TC = Top Centre, BL = Below Left, BC = Below Centre, L = Left, R = Right, CL = Centre Left, B/G = Background.

Illustrations

Mark Duffin: 39, 115, 119, 120; Thomas Girard (Good Illustration): 86; Dusan Lakicevic (Beehive Illustration): 18, 24; Gavin Reece (New Division): 43.

Photos

Back cover (woman with whiteboard): Jenny Acheson/Stockbyte/GettyImages; Back cover (whiteboard): Nemida/GettyImages; Back cover (man using phone): Betsie Van Der Meer/Taxi/GettyImages; Back cover (woman smiling): PeopleImages.com/DigitalVision/GettyImages; Back cover (name tag): Tetra Images/GettyImages; Back cover (handshake): David Lees/Taxi/GettyImages; p. v (TL): Hill Street Studios/Blend Images/GettyImages; p. v (BR): Hill Street Studios/Blend Images/GettyImages; p. v (BL): track5/E+/GettyImages; p. v (TR): fstop123/E+/GettyImages; p. 58 (header), p. viii (Unit 9): Dusty Pixel photography/Moment/GettyImages; p. 58 (automotive): Reza Estakhrian/Iconica/GettyImages; p. 58 (car wash): gilaxia/E+/iStock/Getty Images Plus/GettyImages; p. 58 (computer repair): Tetra Images/GettyImages; p. 58 (security repair): fatihhoca/iStock/Getty Images Plus/GettyImages; p. 58 (carpet cleaning): leezsnow/E+/GettyImages; p. 58 (home repair): sturti/E+/GettyImages; p. 58 (laundry cleaning): kali9/E+/GettyImages; p. 58 (tutoring): Hill Street Studios/Blend Images/GettyImages; p. 59 (Jessica): imagenavi/GettyImages; p. 59 (Peter): g-stockstudio/iStock/Getty Images Plus/GettyImages; p. 59 (Barry): Maskot/GettyImages; p. 59 (Tricia): Andersen Ross/GettyImages; p. 60: MachineHeadz/iStock/Getty Images Plus/GettyImages; p. 61: Morsa Images/DigitalVision/GettyImages; p. 62 (L): James And James/Photolibrary/GettyImages; p. 62 (C): Jose Luis Pelaez Inc/Blend Images/GettyImages; p. 62 (R): Dan Dalton/Caiaimage/GettyImages; p. 63: Paul Morigi/Getty Images Entertainment/Getty Images North America/GettyImages; p. 64 (header), p. viii (Unit 10): Kimberley Coole/Lonely Planet Images/GettyImages; p. 64 (1975): Jason Todd/DigitalVision/GettyImages; p. 64 (1982): Photofusion/Universal Images Group Editorial/GettyImages; p. 64 (1996): Kimberly Butler/The LIFE Images Collection/GettyImages; p. 64 (2004): Graffizone/E+/GettyImages; p. 64 (2006): Future Publishing/Future/GettyImages; p. 64 (2013): Jacob Ammentorp Lund/iStock/Getty Images Plus/GettyImages; p. 65 (T): Mark Dadswell/Getty Images Sport/Getty Images AsiaPac/GettyImages; p. 65 (B): andresr/E+/GettyImages; p. 66: Steve Sands/FilmMagic/GettyImages; p. 67 (T): Walter Bibikow/AWL Images/GettyImages; p. 67 (B): ferrantraite/Vetta/GettyImages; p. 68 (BR): JGI/Jamie Grill/Blend Images/GettyImages; p. 68 (crossing slackline): Ascent Xmedia/The Image Bank/GettyImages; p. 69 (B/G): vladimir zakharov/Moment/GettyImages; p. 69: PASIEKA/Science Photo Library/GettyImages; p. 70: Jonas Gratzer/LightRocket/GettyImages; p. 71 (T): NASA/The LIFE Picture Collection/GettyImages; p. 71 (B): Hero Images/GettyImages; p. 72 (header), p. viii (Unit 11): Hero Images/GettyImages; p. 72 (T): PeopleImages/DigitalVision/GettyImages; p. 72 (B): Hero Images/GettyImages; p. 73: martinedoucet/E+/GettyImages; p. 74: Jamie Kingham/Image Source/GettyImages; p. 75 (L): Rick Gomez/Blend Images/GettyImages; p. 75 (R): Simon Winnall/Taxi/GettyImages; p. 76: Elenathewise/iStock/Getty Images Plus/GettyImages; p. 77 (R): FilippoBacci/E+/GettyImages; p. 77 (L): Comstock Images/Stockbyte/GettyImages; p. 78 (header), p. viii (Unit 12): Jose Luis Pelaez Inc/Blend Images/GettyImages; p. 78: Martin Barraud/Caiaimage/GettyImages; p. 79: Martin Poole/The Image Bank/GettyImages; p. 80 (T): Tim Roberts/GettyImages; p. 80 (B): Chris Ryan/Caiaimage/GettyImages; p. 81: Anadolu Agency/Anadolu/GettyImages; p. 82: Car Culture/Car Culture®Collection/GettyImages; p. 83 (T): UpperCut Images/GettyImages; p. 84: Tetra Images/GettyImages; p. 85: ullstein bild/GettyImages; p. 86 (header), p. viii (Unit 13): Manfred Gottschalk/Lonely Planet Images/GettyImages; p. 86: Image Source/GettyImages; p. 87 (L): James Lauritz/Photodisc/GettyImages; p. 87 (R): RichLegg/E+/GettyImages; p. 88 (T): Sweet Wedding/GettyImages; p. 88 (B): Gogosvm/iStock/Getty Images Plus/GettyImages; p. 89: LisaValder/E+/GettyImages; p. 91 (T): serdjophoto/iStock/Getty Images Plus/GettyImages; p. 91 (B): Ian Cuming/Ikon Images/GettyImages; p. 92 (header), p. viii (Unit 14): bjones27/E+/GettyImages; p. 92 (BR): GUILLAUME SOUVANT/AFP/GettyImages; p. 93 (T): GUILLAUME SOUVANT/AFP/GettyImages; p. 93 (B): Highwaystarz-Photography/iStock/Getty Images Plus/GettyImages; p. 94 (TL): B. O'Kane/Alamy; p. 94 (TC): Hill Street Studios/Blend Images/GettyImages; p. 94 (TR): Tom and Steve/Moment/GettyImages; p. 94 (CL): Daniela White Images/Moment/GettyImages; p. 94 (C): Lucia Lambriex/Taxi/GettyImages; p. 94 (CR): Caiaimage/Sam Edwards/OJO+/GettyImages; p. 94 (B): Hero Images/GettyImages; p. 95 (TL): Mads Perch/Iconica/GettyImages; p. 95 (TR): Plume Creative/DigitalVision/GettyImages; p. 95 (BL): Sam Edwards/Caiaimage/GettyImages; p. 95 (BR): asiseeit/E+/GettyImages; p. 96: Gary Houlder/Taxi/GettyImages; p. 97 (R): FREDERICK FLORIN/AFP/GettyImages; p. 97 (L): Tim Robberts/The Image Bank/GettyImages; p. 98: Image Source/GettyImages; p. 99 (TL): Vico Collective/Michael Shay/Blend Images/GettyImages; p. 99 (TR): Eric Audras/ONOKY/GettyImages; p. 99 (BR): Morsa Images/DigitalVision/GettyImages; p. 100 (header), p. viii (Unit 15): 04linz/iStock/GettyImages; p. 100: Joe McBride/Stone/GettyImages; p. 101: Boston Globe/GettyImages; p. 102 (T): Toby Burrows/DigitalVision/GettyImages; p. 102 (B): andipantz/iStock/GettyImages; p. 103: Maskot/GettyImages; p. 104: John Lund/Marc Romanelli/Blend Images/GettyImages; p. 105: Commercial Eye/The Image Bank/GettyImages; p. 106 (header), p. viii (Unit 16): David Trood/Stone/GettyImages; p. 106 (T): Hero Images/GettyImages; p. 106 (B/G): Klaus Vedfelt/DigitalVision/GettyImages; p. 106 (B): Tetra Images - Daniel Grill/Brand X Pictures/GettyImages; p. 107: Tara Moore/Taxi/GettyImages; p. 108: Ariel Skelley/Blend Images/GettyImages; p. 109 (T): Lumina Images/Blend Images/GettyImages; p. 109 (B): Nino H. Photography/Moment Open/GettyImages; p. 110 (TL): David Malan/Photographer's Choice/GettyImages; p. 110 (TC): Sam Edwards/OJO Images/GettyImages; p. 110 (TR): m-imagephotography/iStock/Getty Images Plus/GettyImages; p. 110 (BR): John S Lander/LightRocket/GettyImages; p. 111 (T): Samir Hussein/WireImage/GettyImages; p. 111 (B): AFP/GettyImages; p. 112: Zero Creatives/Image Source/GettyImages; p. 113: andresrimaging/iStock/Getty Images Plus/GettyImages; p. 123 (TL): Tetra Images/GettyImages; p. 123 (BR): doble-d/iStock/Getty Images Plus/GettyImages; p. 124 (Frida Kahlo): Michael Ochs Archives/GettyImages; p. 124 (Volkswagen): 8c061bbf_466/iStock Editorial/Getty Images Plus/GettyImages; p. 124 (Alexander): Bettmann/GettyImages; p. 125 (R): jmb_studio/iStock/Getty Images Plus/GettyImages; p. 125 (L): jmb_studio/iStock/Getty Images Plus/GettyImages; p. 125 (backpack): Songbird839/iStock/Getty Images Plus/GettyImages; p. 125 (dollar jar): IcemanJ/iStock/Getty Images Plus/GettyImages; p. 125 (balls): Ian McKinnell/Photographer's Choice/GettyImages; p. 125 (chips): MarkGillow/E+/GettyImages; p. 125 (video game): Angelo Angeles/Hemera/Getty Images Plus/GettyImages; p. 126 (L): Stuart Dee/Photographer's Choice/GettyImages; p. 126 (C): Riccardo Livorni/EyeEm/GettyImages; p. 126 (R): 3D_generator/iStock/Getty Images Plus/GettyImages; p. 127: Daviles/iStock/Getty Images Plus/GettyImages; p. 128 (photo 1a): Carl Court/Getty Images News/Getty Images Europe/GettyImages; p. 128 (photo 1b): Helen H. Richardson/Denver Post/GettyImages; p. 128 (photo 2a): GabryC/iStock/Getty Images Plus/GettyImages; p. 128 (photo 2b): Tom Merton/Hoxton/GettyImages; p. 128 (photo 3a): Multi-bits/The Image Bank/GettyImages; p. 128 (photo 3b): Stuart O'Sullivan/The Image Bank/GettyImages; p. 128 (photo 4a): scyther5/iStock/Getty Images Plus/GettyImages; p. 128 (photo 4b): Bread and Butter Productions/The Image Bank/GettyImages; p. 129 (TR): Dave J Hogan/Getty Images Entertainment/Getty Images Europe/GettyImages; p. 129 (CL): Dan Istitene/Getty Images Sport/Getty Images Europe/GettyImages; p. 129 (CR): Allen Berezovsky/WireImage/GettyImages; p. 129 (BL): Fred Stein Archive/Archive Photos/GettyImages; p. 129 (BR): Bettmann/GettyImages; p. 130 (L): Image Source/GettyImages; p. 130 (C): Jen Grantham/iStock Editorial/Getty Images Plus/GettyImages; p. 130 (R): Mauro Speziale/The Image Bank/GettyImages; p. 131: Jay Reilly/UpperCut Images/GettyImages.